Houston, We Have a Possum

Further Observations from a Working Poet

*Poets notice what other people miss.
Nationally-known poet Molly Fisk's singular
perspective on love, death, grammar, lingerie,
small towns, marsupials, and the rest of the natural
world will get you laughing, crying, and thinking.*

Houston, We Have a Possum

Further Observations from a Working Poet

Molly Fisk

Story Street Press
Nevada City, California
2016

Published by Story Street Press
10068 Newtown Rd.
Nevada City, CA 95959
e-mail: molly@mollyfisk.com
www.mollyfisk.com

This edition was produced for on-demand distribution by
ingramspark.com and createspace.com for Story Street Press.

Cover design: Maxima Kahn
Cover photo: Aefa Mullholland
Cover possum: Morag, a wild resident of Toronto, Canada
Author photo: Aeron Miller Photography
Typesetting: Wordsworth (wordsworthofmarin.com)
Technical Support: Paul Emery, Steve Baker, Shawna Hein
13-and-Under Inspiration: Elinor, Zoe, Merren, and Geo LeVell
14-and-Over Inspiration: Robert Lee Haycock, Sam Fisk, Heidi
LeVell, Shannon Francis Schott
Natation Inspiration: Sandy Frizzell, Pat Sharp, Nancy Burns
Contributing Caffienation: Sierra Mountain Coffee Roasters,
Curly Wolf Espresso House, Three Forks Bakery and Brewery,
Kate Dwyer & Jacquie Bellon
Frequency: KVMR 89.5 FM Nevada City, CA (105.1 Truckee,
104.7 Woodland, 88.3 Placerville, kvmr.org), The California
Report, KQED 88.5 FM San Francisco, CA (89.3 Sacramento)

© 2016 by Molly Fisk

All rights reserved. No portion of this book may be reproduced or transmitted in any form or by any means, electronic or mechanical, including photocopying or recording, or by any information storage or retrieval system, without permission in writing from the publisher.

Printed in the United States of America

978-0-9894958-3-7

Dedicated to my favorite possum:

Gioia Fisk

Also by Molly Fisk

poetry:

The More Difficult Beauty
Listening to Winter
Terrain (with Dan Bellm & Forrest Hamer)
Salt Water Poems (letterpress by Jungle Garden Press)

essays/radio commentary:

Using Your Turn Signal Promotes World Peace (book)
"Using Your Turn Signal Promotes World Peace" (CD)
Blow-Drying a Chicken (book)
"Blow-Drying a Chicken" (CD)

Contents

SPRING FEVER

Entitlement	12
Is the Cup Half-Full?	15
Spring Fever	18
Kissing, Creativity, & Liverwurst	21
Baby Snake Season	24
Enlisted	27
Suggestions	30
Growing Up	33
Jealousy Is Your Friend	36
Please, No More Chickens!!	39
Chin-Ups & Devotion	43
Different Strokes	46
It's Curtains	49

BECAUSE AUGUST

The Fisks Do Not Like Vinegar	54
Mowing	57
I See the Moon and the Moon Sees Me	60
Hating Summer	63
The Compost Pile	66
Houston, We Have a Possum	69
Nowhere to Hide	72
Because August	75
Piles of Tomatoes on the Highway	78
The Width of Nevada	81
Giftiness	84
Possum 1, Poet 0	87

SPENDING DAYLIGHT

Ready for Anything?	92
Give Me a Break	95

Spending Daylight	98
A Dark Night in the Daytime	101
Now That I'm Fat	104
Deadwood	107
More Than Your John Hancock	110
The Color of My Car	113
Trimming Season	116
On Not Becoming a Ballerina	119
Normal Every-Day Sloth & Torpor	122
How to Avoid a Boring Life	125

A WHITER SHADE OF PALE

The Swans	130
Reindeer	133
Duck Potholders & Galoises	136
Balloon Up Your Nose!	139
A Whiter Shade of Pale	142

The Watusi	145
Ursus Californiensis	148
Borrowing Other Mothers	151
Glass Houses	154
Valentine Grumblings	157
The Gates	160
Wedding Bells	163
Acknowledgements	167
About the Author	169

SPRING FEVER

Entitlement

I don't know about you, but I hate doing what I'm supposed to. The idea of being good gets under my skin and makes me want to swear loudly in public or drive the wrong way down a one-way street.

This came up as I watched myself glide through a stop sign in third gear this morning. My rationale is that since the stop sign didn't used to be there, and I didn't *used* to have to stop, I don't have to stop now. That makes sense, doesn't it? If someone else gave me this argument I would be rolling my eyeballs. There's just a part of me that doesn't want to obey the rules. I drive along the back of a local supermarket, where all the loading trucks are, to miss the speed bumps in front, and feel as though I have special privileges. *I'm cool, I know a shortcut.*

Do you ever feel this way? I'm extremely good in most situations: I'm polite, I put my napkin in my lap and meet almost all of my deadlines. I never litter. I take paint cans to the special place at the dump where paint cans go. But all the while, the part of my brain that wears too much mascara and a black leather jacket is looking for a sneaky way around the rules.

I don't know where this sense of entitlement comes from, although it may be hereditary: my dad had it in spades. Is my life boring and I'm trying to create a little risk, a scintilla of drama, by tempting invisible highway patrolpersons at that stop sign? Did I never get past the teenage rebellion stage? I'm 60 years old. My parents are dead. Exactly which grown-ups are going to reprimand me?

Being good just seems exhausting. I'm always being good. When do I get to be bad? Don't you sometimes want to buy a can of spray paint and go wild? And I don't mean spraying lines from poems on the side of a warehouse, which *could* be considered art. I mean 10-foot high bright red curses dripping down the front of City Hall.

What keeps me from acting out these urges is that I'd *so* hate to be caught. I don't like it when people are mad at me. I never cruise through that stop sign if there's a cop in sight, and believe me, I do look around. The Pepperidge Farm driver asking me to get the heck out of the way is one thing, I can take it. But what if someone I know saw me spraying graffiti on the Episcopal Church at two in the morning, or picking every rose out of a front yard? I'd probably be arrested. Semi-Famous Local Poet Defaces Historic Landmark. Can you imagine? I'd never live it down.

So I limit myself to parking in yellow zones before six o'clock and slipping in the back doors of restaurants. Returning library books after the due date. Boldly taking my own popcorn to the movies. It's ridiculous, but I can't seem to stop wanting to be special. Even though my political and spiritual philosophies both tell me that everyone's equal, some days, I don't want to be equal.

Some days I just want to be King.

Is the Cup Half-Full?

Last year I planted two crabapple trees in my yard. One blooms pale pink, the other a deep magenta. Don't ask me what their names are, I'm sure I have the little tags in my junk drawer but I never remember information like that. Both trees are just about to pop, and I'm feeling as wealthy as the Sultan of Brunei.

Isn't it strange what makes the cup look half-full? Two weeks ago I was ready to cancel my health insurance and rent out my house for a month just for the extra cash, and now I'm swaggering around the yard conversing with fruit trees. Nothing much changed in the intervening weeks. Somebody paid an old bill I thought I'd never see. It doesn't amount to enough money to placate Blue Cross, but it turned my world sunny-side up.

My mother was wonderful but she had a tendency toward pessimism, especially where her kids were concerned. We had to invent a new verb to describe this — "catastrophize." On the least provocation, she would launch into a Rolodex of fears about what one of us was planning to do. None of this you-are-wonderful-and-capable-have-fun-trying-this-new-thing for her. It was you've-got-to-be-careful,-this-could-be-dangerous,-are-you-sure-you're-ready,-I-don't-think-this-is-a-good-idea-at-*all*.

In contrast, my father sold pork belly futures over the phone at 6 a.m. from his waterbed. Need I say more? His boundless optimism was just as unrealistic as my mother's trepidation. So I come by my flip-flopping view of the world quite honestly. The question is, how to find the middle ground?

Two of my friends are students of Buddhism. They encourage me to rein in my projections and if I'm having a bad day, let it be confined to right now instead of forecasting my suffering into the next decade. They also recommend considering a wider context — looking back a few centuries does take the sting out of one Blue Cross bill.

Some people make gratitude lists or propose that serving others in small ways can neutralize the pessimistic voices in our heads, as well as the self-aggrandizement. What tends to work best for me is to ride whichever wave I'm on to its most extreme conclusion. "I'll never write another poem, I'll spend my 70s living in a culvert, I'm a born loser."

Following the optimism is harder, because, like many people, I secretly hope for miracles. But it still works: I'm bound to win a Pulitzer Prize for my next book, and then a MacArthur grant, and fall in love with someone tomorrow while we're waiting in the check-out-line of the grocery store.

Half an hour of this silliness and I can usually muster a little more perspective.

And sometimes, when the sun comes out after a week of rain and my crabapple buds are bursting, a kind of wild joy rips through me, a reward for all the times when life is hard.

Spring Fever

Welcome to April. The sky is blue, the grass is green, birds are singing, and it's just warm enough to take off your sweater. The plum trees are dropping their petals; the dark pink crabapple blooms are half-open; the pears are ready to burst; the real apple blossoms are still tight on their branches, biding their time. Wherever I walk in my yard there's a sound of bees, which I take as a very good omen since bees have been so hard-hit by disease and climate change in recent years.

If you're a person who likes sex, spring is your season. Tulips erupt out of the ground like you-know-what, and then unfurl their gorgeous lapped petals to reveal tantalizing inner views like you-know-what-else. Every living thing is calling out for attention: Look at *me*! Come over *here*! Smell *this*! Touch *right there*! Meanwhile the breeze has warmed and the air is softer, waking our skin to sensation again after those long months swathed in polypropylene or wool.

The bombardment of sensory input is enough to make anyone swoon, and that's exactly what it's designed for: Spring is nature's way of keeping the game going. Replicate that DNA! Pollinate those trees! It's like an orgy, but out in public where everyone can enjoy it. There's a reason they call it Spring Fever, too: it's definitely catching. I'm surprised more people aren't making out in front of City Hall and removing each others' clothes in the middle of Broad St. If we were in Paris (don't you wish we were in Paris?), there would certainly be more kissing. The people of that city spend a fantastic amount of time locking lips with each other. But I digress. Spring wants you to digress. Little breezes waft past and you follow them to see what that lovely scent is — lilac? jonquil?

If you had told me when I was young that people of my current age thought about sex in the springtime, I would have been horrified. More than that, I just wouldn't have believed you. My world view, like that of many young people today, capped sexual activity at about age 38. This is slowly changing, of course, helped along by our sexy soon-to-be-ex-President and First Lady, who actually nuzzle in public, and as Brad and Angelina get older. But the idea that lots and *lots* of people in their 50s, 60s, 70s, and 80s are not just thinking about sex but are actually *having* it is slow to be absorbed by the younger generation. That's OK with me — they should be thinking about their own sex lives, not wondering what their grandparents' friends are up to in bed.

In springtime, their grandparents' friends probably aren't in bed, anyway, they're having sex in meadows or the spacious back seats of late-model Lincolns with the windows rolled down to let in some fresh air. They're being egged on by the sound and smell and taste and texture of every other living thing.

So what are you doing reading a book? Hop to it!

Kissing, Creativity, & Liverwurst

One of the things that happens when you're a poet is that people come up to you at silent auctions and board meetings, or in line at the movies — anywhere you might be standing around — and ask you questions about your work. The questions themselves are sort of incoherent, and not that important, it's what's behind them that's interesting. Almost every time, what people want to know is how I learned to be so creative, and how they can learn, too.

Little kids would never ask me this because they're still bursting with creativity, it's completely natural to them. But somewhere along the road to socialization, via high school, college, paychecks, smog tests, mortgages, and the other responsibilities of modern life, creativity tends to get lost and we have to find it again.

Luckily, it's not that hard. Creativity is about your essence, whether you express it in poems, paintings, dance, fiddle-music, really great lasagne, or perfectly timed wisecracks. The way to become creative is to start being yourself as deeply as possible.

This distillation is a life-long process, but it's easy to begin. Walk around your town and have opinions about things. What do you think of that wrought-iron fence, this billboard, those climbing roses? Don't say anything out loud — you don't want to be mean. I would never tell someone that his socks were a terrible color…well, actually, I might, but only if we were friends. The reason to do this is to find out who you are. Do you like the window display in this bookstore? The smell wafting out of that café? Why? Why not? What do you like most, and least?

Color matters enormously to me, and I love the proportions of 18th and 19th century buildings, the gingerbread and mullions. That big white house at the top of Broad St. pleases my eye, and I think the government complex off Highway 49 is hideous.

Maybe you're someone who could care less about houses and color but can identify motorcycles by make and year just hearing them chug up a hill. Go ahead, leave your desk and walk around for half an hour, finishing this sentence over and over: "I am

a person who loves or can't stand…dot, dot, dot…"
Do you hate contrived exercises like this? Are you someone who'd rather gaze into a computer screen than take a walk? Do you like numbers? Do you like snakes? What bores you? Who are you? The more you can find out about yourself, the more creativity will start to churn in your brain.

Me, I like standing under trees and looking up through the leaves at flickering shards of sunlight. I hate comedy but love wit, cleverness, and wordplay. I hate liverwurst and muggy weather. Hugs used to make me very uncomfortable. They don't any more, but I still prefer kissing. I could kiss for days.

Baby Snake Season

Even though we've gotten very little winter in my town this year and everyone's worried about drought, spring has unequivocally arrived. All the fruit and nut trees are blooming at once, the daffodils are up, grape hyacinth, magnolias, camellias, forsythia...The flowering quince are still hanging in, those shades of dark coral bright against tiny green leaves. Next up are dogwoods and lilacs, and everything I forget about until spring rolls around again.

The cats I live with know it's spring because there are different birds on the lawn. A lot of teeth-chattering attention through window glass is being paid to robins and titmice, Mountain Bluebirds and Red-Wing blackbirds.

But the real harbinger of spring in my mind is the baby snake. Not every household pays attention to baby snakes, but if you have any cats who were abandoned in and then rescued from a barn in San Luis Obispo, you'll know what I mean. I never see the snakes arrive, although I'd bet it's Gracie, my 16-year-old, half-blind, 7 lb. hunter who catches them. They just materialize on the kitchen tiles, gorgeous slim green or black pieces of string, all muscle no matter how tiny. As you know, cats like to play with their food. But snakes are slippery, wily, and astonishingly fast. And I don't think they taste good, or the cats wouldn't let them slither under book cases and refrigerators quite so quickly.

I have been den mother, nursemaid, and entire downstairs staff to at least two cats for the last 25 years, and once, briefly, as many as nine. Over this time I've learned to put hot compresses on abscessed wounds, clean up any number of bodily fluids and solids, dispose of half-eaten squirrels, save birds from feline jaws, and pick up baby snakes.

I'm not generally afraid of snakes, but I don't feel relaxed with them, either. I've held my neighbor's pet King snake, who's at least four feet long and two inches around, but only because he named her Betty, and I didn't want to lose face. It's patently ridiculous to fear anyone named Betty. Snakes are essentially one long muscle. It's amazing to feel them inching down your arm behind that

iconic wedge-shaped head and a forked tongue
delicately flicking in and out to taste the air.

These teeny snakes I pick up sort of by the neck,
in hopes they can't then turn their heads and bite
me. Sometimes they curl up like Christmas ribbons
or thrash around, but mostly they hang suspended
like a stick, taut and wary. I lay them down in the
flower beds, and my cats for some reason don't
follow me outside, but sniff and hunt through the
kitchen, completely mystified about where the little
darlings have gone. This makes it criminally easy
to outwit them, which is good, because right now
it's five against one around here, and I need all the
advantage I can get.

The only thing that worries me is what will
happen when my refrigerator dies and I need to
install a new one. There might be 212 tiny shriveled
bodies under there. Or maybe just one really big live
one.

Enlisted

I've been making lists every morning for 45 years with the same result: some things get done and some don't. I've written them in notebooks, on calendars, blackboards, bank deposit envelopes, and recently into my telephone. Sometimes I name the lists *Tuesday* or *Friday*, *Big List,* or *Don't Forget*. In college I used calligraphy markers from an architectural supply store. Today it's a brown Uniball Signo I bought in San Francisco's Japantown because that's the only place I can find a .38 thickness — the U.S.-made ones only go down to .5.

Some of you are nodding your heads and thinking of the kind of pen you use. Many more are screwing up your faces in disbelief that anyone would care. But a pen is one of the few tools of my trade. Surgeons, painters, mechanics have a vast array of implements to play with. My pen is scalpel, socket wrench, and boar-bristle filbert brush all rolled into one. I get to be as finicky about its characteristics as any jockey adjusting the height of her stirrups.

But I digress, which is why I made a list in the first place — to remind me of what's important today. "Call Rex" is the opening salvo. My car needs new shocks — Rex is my mechanic. "Draft essay" is next, which you can see is underway. "Update readings" means that page on my website needs attention. I'm inexpert at editing my website, so items like this are sometimes done last or maybe next week. "Wash little rugs" has been on every list I've made since New Year's, and they're still in a pile by my front door.

One of the problems, at least for someone with complicated feelings about authority and obedience, is how great a set-up lists are for rebellion. The minute a task is written down it becomes fair game for avoidance, resentment, projection, and general misery. This is how most of us learn that putting something off takes much more time than just doing it. I know you know what I mean.

I usually start making a list with great optimism and end it feeling tired. I cram enough on one day's list to fill a week and then can't imagine how I'm going to get it done. My friend Julia once added

as her last item: "Save the world," which made
us both laugh but also pointed out she might be
asking a little too much of herself. Another mistake
is not to break tasks down into single action items.
On my list it says "BOOKS!!!" with exclamation
marks, clear signs of hysteria. More useful is "Take
unwanted books from shelves and put in box." "Put
box in car." "Drive to library donation drop-off."

Some days I make a list that just says "Breathe,"
or "Smile." Some incredibly lucky days I can turn
my list into a poem.

Suggestions

One of my friends' kids has done something
fabulous. He's a grade-school teacher in Manhattan,
and, with a friend, walked around New York City
carrying a huge white box that said Suggestions
on the side of it, asking people if they wanted to
make a suggestion. About anything. I'm not sure
what I would do if approached by two guys and a
big white box, but a lot of the people they met sat
on park benches or leaned against buildings and
wrote suggestions. Otis (the kid) and his friend
had brought along some clipboards to make this
easier, which also may have allayed any nervousness
passersby would be tempted to feel about two
guys and a box. Somehow the sight of a clipboard
banishes thoughts of rape and pillaging, at least in
my mind. There's something comforting and earnest
about them: they conjure up things like petitions for
more trees in your neighborhood.

A lot of people made suggestions. Some were political, some personal, some civic. When they took the box to the Brooklyn Bridge, a man wrote "It's a nice bridge, but would it be too much to give it a lick of paint?" Otis tells a story of getting suggestions from a mother and young son. The son wrote that he thought all children should be able to go to summer camp, and the mother looked at him in astonishment, saying, "I didn't know you wanted to go to camp!"

A Spanish-speaking woman wrote that there should be a universal passport, so people could travel from one country to another any time they wanted. Somebody wrote that she thought Jonathan should kiss her. Jonathan turned out to be reading over her shoulder, and took her suggestion on the spot. There were suggestions to get out of Iraq, that men should treat their women better, that "David should stop bugging me and get a life." There were a lot of suggestions involving beer. Otis's mom's favorite suggestion is one that somebody wrote, scribbled out so you can't read it, and then dropped in the box.

I am completely in love with the way this process solicits the opinions of ordinary people. Reading the suggestions made me want to cry. They were so honest: heartfelt, bizarre, and completely personal. It made me think of true democracy, that old idea of hearing from absolutely everyone.

These suggestions have been collected into a book, in their original handwriting, which will be published by *Chronicle*. Otis' mom and I are both writers, and we are mildly jealous that this kid has a book coming out and we don't, and that it's such a great book. But mostly we are pleased as punch. Otis and his friend think up interactive public art projects under the name Illegal Art. I can't wait to see what they come up with next. I have more than half a mind to move to New York and join them.

My favorite suggestion was noteworthy both for its crass enthusiasm and its cutting-edge novelty: "Beer-flavored nipples!"

Now that's art.

Growing Up

This week I've been contemplating the idea of being a grown-up. You know: doing what needs to be done, doing your share, taking responsibility, and not complaining. If there's one time of the year tailor-made for this, it's the first week of April.

For many years all I felt in early April was fear. "Oh, no," I'd think. "I haven't done my taxes. I'd better do my taxes. They can't be late. They can't be wrong. What if I make a mistake? Where will I get the money to pay them? What if that time I cheated in 1983 gets found out?" I was a quivering mass of anxiety — it's a wonder my signature on the 1040 was legible at all.

Back before computers, citizens like me sat at kitchen tables and filled the forms out in pencil. When we were totally sure the numbers were correct, we copied them over in black ink. We used adding machines (with paper tape, no less) or calculators to do the math. And before those were invented, people like my parents just did the math long-hand on a piece of paper. Then we went to the local copy shop to xerox the whole darn thing and sent it in about 10 p.m. on April 15, waiting in line with hundreds of other people at the local post office, which was open that one night until midnight. It was kind of a national party by that time — you saw your neighbors in line, people loaned each other pens to write return addresses and quarters if someone was short for stamps.

Since then I've participated in tax day from almost every angle. I've paid early, on time, late, and not at all. I've gotten extensions, paid on the installment plan, delighted in refunds and owed big fines. I've hired accountants, done it myself, used TurboTax, and been so poor there was no reason to file. I've been audited. I've cried in frustration, giggled with relief, and been bored at the whole ridiculous proceeding. And always there's been that frisson of fear in the back of my mind. "I'm not doing it right, and I'm going to get caught and punished."

This year, something has changed. Maybe I'm finally old enough not to be scared of bureaucracy. Maybe because I've had every tax experience known to mankind except jail time and princely wealth, I know the territory now. Or perhaps I've just learned to love myself enough that I'm not really afraid of anything. This year, dealing with my taxes was simply problem-solving. "What did I spend? How much is the tax? Will I have enough cash to pay it or do I need to do installments?" There was an equanimity to the process I've never experienced before. I wasn't a bad person for not using Quicken. I had all my receipts in two manilla envelopes. I got out my registers and made lists of what I'd spent in each category. Added them up. I wasn't a bad person for spending what I'd spent. I wasn't a bad person for disliking having to meet an official deadline, nor for not having enough money to open an IRA. I just did the work, plugged it into TurboTax, and filed. I mailed the checks early because the interest rate on what I owed wasn't enough to keep a mouse in crumbs — waiting until the last minute made no sense.

Not to say that I felt no emotion. I actually felt quite a lot. But it wasn't fear, it was anger. While I'm using up an entire weekend and paying seven percent of my very small annual income to the United States of America, most huge corporations are not. They're letting poets and all the rest of us pay their way for them.

I'm thinking perhaps they need a little encouragement to grow up.

Jealousy Is Your Friend

I haven't always been a poet. For a long time
I didn't know what to be, and worked in clothing
stores, engineering/architecture joint ventures, and
swank French restaurants. I ran a knitting business
for seven years, making Scandinavian-style sweaters
with pterodactyls on them instead of reindeer. I
went to business school at 30 and passed as a banker
— a Fortune 1000 lender in Chicago, no less — for
three years before I realized I was only pretending I
could stand it.

During this time my mother sat happily at the
kitchen table after her nursing shift ended, drawing
flowers in vases or the faces of people she knew
from church: exquisite line drawings that captured
delicate petals and subtleties of expression. My Aunt
Mary had painted most of her life, and was getting
good gallery shows. Her daughter Liz taught at an
art school, her son Michael sculpted his own work as

well as innovative serving utensils for a tableware company, and my youngest cousin, Miranda, did life-like paintings of people's dogs and houses for a living.

I don't know how you interpret jealousy in your life, but for years I saw it as a moral failing: something to be ashamed of and eradicate. Then a poet-friend torqued my thinking. "Jealousy is one of the best ways to find out what you want to do next! It points you in new directions." The next day I visited my sister, the organizational development consultant, and there on her wall was the gorgeous print of dolphins she made in college.

"I want to make art!!" I growled to myself on the drive home. "Writing is boring! My eyes are falling asleep. I want to play with color too! Everyone else in this dang family can do it, why not me?" This isn't strictly true, since I have one brother whose artistry is mainly, like our dad, in his incredibly good taste in clothes, and also a brother and cousin who both write but don't paint. But you get the idea.

Jealousy isn't only an indicator of what to try next, it's a wonderful fuel for action. Four years later, I'm spending Monday afternoons with people who smell deliciously of turpentine. Everyone's painting something different. I was originally fixated on water in mason jars, because it's hard to capture. Then I moved on to barns, and now boats. In time-honored artistic tradition, I'm copying the work of other people and trying to figure out how they do it. Where does light hit glass? How does a boat's shape change when it's reflected in rippling water?

My first efforts were decidedly wonky, but now I'm getting the hang of it. A few friends have actually *bought* some of my work. I'm happy to let them, despite feeling like a total fraud. It's very fun to make something and then get paid for it a few days later — an experience poets do not generally have — but I would never call myself a painter.

I'm still a poet, but one who — by the unexpected grace of envy — is learning to paint.

Please, No More Chickens!!

Once upon a time, last spring, I started my usual joky schtick on Facebook about how many shopping days remained until my birthday. This is a line from the comic strip Peanuts. It's a better joke if the number of days is many, so I try to start mentioning this at least two months ahead.

People say no one is real on Facebook, we're all trying to put our best feet forward, toward the idyllic rather than the ordinary. I certainly see more photos of anniversary dinners than divorce-court waiting rooms, but personally, I try to add in how I really feel as much as I can. I'm not a fan of faking things.

I was going to turn 60 in July, and how I felt about that was astonished. I had no expectation I'd be living this long, and there was a sweetness surrounding the idea that put me in a good mood for months.

However, I was also very aware of a certain Facebook trifecta: the fact that I once wrote a book with "chicken" in the title, the fact that since I'm a poet I have 5000 Facebook friends, and the fact that I'm sent an enormous number of chicken-related jokes, stories, photos, and paraphernalia on a regular basis. People began to ask what I wanted for my birthday, such an auspicious year, etc., and all I could see was a parade of plastic chickens arriving at my front door. I don't actually subscribe to barnyard idolatry, so somehow I had to head this potential disaster off at the pass.

Over the years I've discovered fabulous benefits to being single, but one of the drawbacks, sexist though it will sound, is that no one gives you jewelry. Since I'm a casual dresser, this isn't a huge problem, but once in a while I do look longingly at an out-of-my-budget gem and sigh.

Sometime in early May these thoughts stopped ricocheting separately around in my head and coalesced, prompting me to declare on social media that if you really wanted to know what I'd like for my birthday, it was a specific pearl ring made by the designer Jamie Joseph in Seattle. I posted a photo, told people how they could contribute, and then got such a stomach ache I had to go lie down.

I don't think the words "will you please buy me that" have ever crossed my lips, not even about a cup of coffee. If something's offered, I've finally learned to say yes, but it's taken me 60 years. I was so embarrassed I'd done this, I almost deleted the post every time I opened my laptop.

But I also began to wake up in a new way. My close friends helped a lot, saying over and over: "what would you do if it were someone *else's* ask?" No question, I'd donate a small amount. I love donating small amounts to all sorts of people and causes. I wouldn't think she was weird, or greedy, or shallow, or entitled. I'd be glad to know what she wanted, so I wasn't giving her that 18th pair of ill-fitting chicken socks made by child-slaves in China or something else absurd. I'd like being part of a group, too, gathering to support a friend.

The big surprise, though, was how much I started to feel engaged in a radical act. Talking about money, asking for what you want, pulling the shame out of those equations as you do it, is bucking cultural norms in a big way. I could tell because of the frequency of my stomach aches. Some of my friends had stomach aches too, they told me later, and others wrote to say they hated watching me do this. I empathized with them all.

In the end, 35 of my Facebook friends contributed to the successful purchase of the ring I'm wearing right now on my writing hand. I love its creamy full-moon shape, the perfect image for a poet. It feels good on my finger. And it's a wonderful reminder that whether you're 60 or single or anything else, the world contains people who want you to be happy.

But to discover this, you have to figure out what you want.

And then you have to ask for it.

Horrible, isn't it?!?

Chin-Ups & Devotion

The other day I ate lunch with a friend I've had for 40 years, and our conversation meandered around to the idea of practicing. We're both life coaches. Julie leans a bit more toward the executive and business end of things, I lean toward relationships, personal growth, and trauma-recovery, but we teach a lot of the same ideas and tools to our clients.

She said she first learned about practicing when she was 11. She was pretty bad in gym, and so was one other girl. They often ended up trading last place in races. I was floored to hear this: Julie's the most athletic person I know! She swam competitively in high school, worked as a professional river guide, and has won Master cross-country ski races for years. She's about to get her black belt in Aikido.

At a test in gym, back in the sixth grade, Julie could not do one single pull-up, but her fellow last-place buddy could do five of them. "I asked her how she knew how to do pull-ups, and she told me she had brothers who would never let her get away with not knowing how to do pull-ups. So she used their chin-up bar and practiced." This was a revelation to Julie, who walked down to the local hardware store that very day with her allowance and bought a chin-up bar, the kind that you twist in the middle to lengthen or shorten. After screwing it into her bedroom's door frame, she practiced until she could do 15 pull-ups. "And I've been able to do them ever since, until just last year, when I screwed up my shoulder," she said.

    I learned to practice when I was 37, the day someone showed me how to revise a poem. Before that I was a fast learner, quick on the uptake, who could get by without practicing anything. But when I started writing poems in my mid-30's, I really didn't know what I was doing. I was naturally good at some parts of it but not others. An older poet sat me down one day and showed me exactly what words could be changed to make one of my poems stronger, and I got it: the message and the technique. Then I practiced. In poem after poem, I changed all the verbs and then went back and changed all the nouns. I took out metaphors, adjectives, almost all the articles. I made my poems squeak with emptiness, and then carefully added slant rhymes and double meanings, so almost every word works on at least two levels.

I'm not a natural practicer. It can feel boring and repetitive and I want to be done, already! So I have to practice practicing. But I'm so happy with the results! My poems are more interesting and complex. The compassion I practice gets wider and deeper.

One of these days, you might even find me at the local hardware store, buying a chin-up bar. Julie says the marks are still visible in the doorway of her childhood bedroom.

Different Strokes

I've been a writer for 30 years but have not made a living from my creative writing. Only about three people in the country make a living from their own creative writing, and usually it's after the sixth or seventh book. I've made my living from *teaching* creative writing, as well as helping people write resumes, blog posts, wedding vows, and other one-time assignments, and now, also, for the last five years, as that consummate 21st century California cliché, a life coach. About a third of my coaching clients are writers. I help them with planning books, sticking to a schedule, overcoming writer's block, meeting deadlines…stuff like that.

Sometimes, like this morning, I have a little private fit about grammar. How is it possible, I say to myself, that someone could get this far in life and not remember the quotation mark goes OUTSIDE the comma, for Pete's sake?!?! This is what happens when you do something for a long time: you forget that not everyone is spending her morning taking sentences apart. Dental hygienists all over the land are probably saying privately to themselves, *How is it possible that someone could get this far in life and still not FLOSS!!* I have to remind myself that whenever I want to make hard boiled eggs I go look in a cookbook and find out, again, how long to boil them, while any chef and probably every parent has this by heart.

People know what they know, and remember what they remember, and nobody is exactly like you, or, in this case, me. Yet I think many of us walk around town thinking that people are very much like us, and not only know what we know but also would do what we would do. Which is why it's so startling when they suddenly break out and vote differently from us, or make some racist/sexist/chowder-headed remark that we find entirely offensive.

This is a fascinating and humbling feature of the universe, don't you think?

The other thing about life I find interesting is how much the larger world is reflected in the specific and personal moment. Right when you're about to have a very strong opinion regarding

Israel and Palestine, for instance, you can just bet one of your neighbors will put up his new fence eight inches on your side of the property line, and there you are, dealing with issues of territory, cooperation, fairness, and compromise. Not to mention frustration, disappointment, righteous indignation, and the rest of Pandora's Box. I won't get into the specifics of conflict in the Middle East, which I am ill-equipped to discuss, but when two people can't even calmly agree about fence placement, it suddenly makes more sense that whole countries might have a hard time with some of their differences.

The question really isn't "Why are there always wars going on?" it's "How have we not killed each other off already?!?" And for *that*, dear reader, despite being good with words, I'm afraid I have no answer.

It's Curtains

It's probably time to confess I have a few long-standing addictions, and one of them is to ironing. I need to iron something at least once a decade or I don't seem to be able to function. Last time it was a tablecloth for Christmas, 2006. I used my own iron, a blue and white hand-me-down whose internal spray mechanism works — unlike the one I had before, which was my mother's proud purchase in 1961 and scorched everything it saw. I used my own ironing board, too, picked up off the street on trash day in Cambridge in the early '80s.

The occasion yesterday was curtains. I've rented an office downtown, to spare my coaching clients having my cats sit on their laps and drool. It's a sweet little room with many windows. I was so in love with the light that I didn't really think about privacy, and it turns out the existing curtains aren't adequate. Anyone over five foot three can see into my room from the lobby. Not the whole room, but still. What if I were teaching an Aikido move and sprang into view? What if a client needed to jump up and down, to blow off steam? We might scare people.

Over the course of a normal life, one usually has to make some curtains. For the six houses I've lived in as an adult, I've made eight pair, and two long ones to cover door-frames. I got them down from the shelf where they'd been sitting quietly, folded, for at least 15 years. The bag they were in had saved them from fading, so all I had to do was iron out the folds. But alas, I could not open my ironing board. The mechanism you hold down with your thumb to engage the legs, which is probably why it was on the street in the first place, had failed after 35 years. They just don't make things like they used to.

Luckily my friend Susanna has an ironing board that's almost always set up. She's not an addict, but she might as well be, given her fondness for linen napkins and throwing parties. I drove my curtains over to her house, moved the damp linen onto a chair, and began.

That's when I remembered I hate ironing. Even curtains, which are rectangular and have no sleeves. The folds were tenacious. The fabric caught on the iron's cord, trying to topple everything. They looked

perfect lying flat on the board, but the minute
I moved to another section, what was hanging
down showed more creases and I had to redo it.
By the time Susanna and Blitzen got home from
the dog park, I was a wreck and ten curtains hung
innocently on their hangers pretending they'd never
seen a fold in their lives.

Was it worth it? They look great in my office,
which is an excellent outcome. I know my clients
will thank me. But I think you can tell the moment
has arrived.

I'm going to have to find a 12-step program for
ironing.

Sigh.

# BECAUSE AUGUST

The Fisks Do Not Like Vinegar

Recently my sister Sarah turned to me — she was in my kitchen for some reason — and said, with authority: "The Fisks do not like vinegar." She must have been making salad dressing — we don't usually discuss condiments as a rule. She went on talking, but I stood stock still inside my mind and let that wonderful idea wash over me.

I don't like vinegar. I've never liked vinegar. I avoid fermentation whenever possible: pickles, pickled herring, wine, the Korean kimchi that people rave about…I've tried them and disliked them. Vinegar makes me cough. It makes my sister cough, too, apparently. But being of, shall we say, a certain middle-class obedient American vintage where salad is on the menu every night, I have been eating the stuff for nigh on sixty years now.

I just called Sarah, and she doesn't remember saying this at all. I can see the half-turn her shoulders made between my sink and the kitchen island when the sentence rolled off her tongue, one in a hundred other sentences that morning, spinach over here, sunflower seeds there, and she was halfway through slicing a cucumber. Isn't this exactly how life is? Somebody rattles off a statement that changes your life, that you never forget, that you base all your behavior on from that moment forward, and they don't even remember having said it.

Not that I plan to base my future behavior on vinegar. But when she said "The Fisks do not like vinegar," I felt such a rush of belonging. *I am a Fisk. And it's true, I do not like vinegar! We are united! I am not alone!*

The modern world, as you know, can be a lonely place. People live alone, drive their cars alone, eat out alone, look at their cell phones too much, you know the drill. I'm not exempt from this: I'm lonely quite a bit of the time, despite having twice the number of Facebook friends as the population of my rural town, not to mention five cats.

You'd think a person with three hilarious, larger-than-life siblings like mine might have felt as though she belonged to her family, but I tend to forget this. It was wonderful to be reminded I am part of a clan, a people with common characteristics:

big wrists, twinkly eyes, and a strong dislike of vinegar.

As I got off the phone with Sarah this morning, another memory popped into my head. One summer when we were 6 and 7, or 7 and 8, she and I traveled around New England with our grandmother in her swell Volkswagen camper bus. There's a picture of the two of us astride a cannon at Fort Ticonderoga.

Inside the bus's sliding door, our father's mother, Jonnie Fisk, had written a list of rules, which had dishes, bed-making, and teeth-brushing on it. It concluded that you had to try "three polite bites" of any food served to you.

"With the exception," she wrote with her signature green pen, in a fine bold hand, "of sauerkraut."

Mowing

I once took an essay-writing workshop from *San Francisco Chronicle* columnist Adair Lara. She said that if your readers don't like you, you're sunk, and therefore some subjects just don't work, like being a size 6, or having an entourage.

Well, God knows I'm not a size 6, and my entourage is feline, which doesn't count, but I did win a prize the other day. Before you write me off, though, let me add that it was a poetry prize, and therefore marginal — along the lines of winning a spelling bee in Latvian or a recipe contest using only plums and Velveeta. Don't get me wrong, I'm thrilled. But it's not something to dislike me for.

Adair also said that the fastest way into readers' hearts is to admit something embarrassing about yourself. Which brings me to the subject of riding lawn mowers.

Last summer, trying to cope with almost an acre of long grass, I bought a ride mower. I wanted to call it a tractor, which has a charming, Wendell Berry-like, rural cachet, but it was just a totally suburban ride mower. For an amazingly long time I was able to Tom-Sawyer other people into mowing with it. But yesterday the grass was knee-high and no gullible friends were around to save me.

Since the operating instructions were printed on the fender, I was able to turn the darn thing on and drive it around in circles quite successfully. I even figured out how to engage the blade so actual mowing took place. I tootled along, cutting a wide swath, as they say, until most of the grass was shorter. There was just this one little inconvenient hill I had been avoiding, where I had to disobey the instructions and mow from side to side instead of uphill and down, due to three maple trees and the septic tank.

The first two passes across this hill were terrifying but accomplished without incident. Traveling at about the speed of grass growing, my non-size-6 person listing perilously to starboard, I made the final approach.

You think I fell off, don't you? Well, I didn't. I would *never* fall off a ride mower. Instead, there was a small cracking sound and the steering wheel came off in my hands. Unfazed by this development, the mower kept going, heading straight for the largest maple.

That was when, with the speed and agility of a bareback stunt rider, I swung one leg over the saddle and slid gracefully to the ground (still gripping the wheel). No, I didn't break anything, and the mower cleverly stopped all by itself. With regal dignity, I jammed the steering wheel back on its column and walked up to the house.

The mower is still out on the lawn. It looks kind of sweet there, red body, black tires, against the green of the grass. Since I'm never going to touch it again, I'm thinking of planting some petunias around the base and calling it yard art.

I See the Moon and the Moon Sees Me

People who work in emergency rooms and police stations know full moons increase their business. Women report that their periods tally with full or new moons, and the ocean tides are completely tethered to the moon. Even my cats go nuts under full moons, chasing each other up trees at two in the morning. I love the moon at any stage, from faint silver thumbnail to fat gold globe rising behind all the spiky pine trees across the street.

So when I was invited to a Women's After-Dark Full-Moon Swim last summer, I went. The moon part and the swim part were right up my alley, and the after-dark part sounded exciting. I had one hesitation, which is that though I love women, I shudder at anything smacking of ritual or ceremony. You will not find me in a circle with a talking stick sharing anything any time soon.

Luckily, the New Age factor was slim to none and the experience was quite moving, so this year I did it again. June's full moon was perfect: warm air, warm water, a few clouds to catch orange light from the sunset but not enough to obscure the rising orb. We were a biggish group, about 15, and joined by some little girls, which made the whole event more fun.

I've always had a fairly sturdy ego. Much of the time, I'm hoping no one realizes just how sturdy, not to say inflated, it is. So there I am, waist deep in a lake with the moon high enough to cast its light over the water, a glittering path right before me. I swim away from shore, into this bright road, thinking how incredibly lucky I am that the moon's rays are directed at me. I feel blessed and grateful. Then I look back toward everyone else, and no moonlit trails extend toward them. I feel sort of curious, and sort of guilty, since I've been having a pretty great life lately and this just seems like icing on the proverbial cake, but I decide to not worry and to enjoy my good fortune while it lasts.

It takes a full ten breast strokes for my self-centered brain to wake up and unravel the mystery. "You, idiot," it says, not unkindly. "Moonlight goes toward whoever is LOOKING at it! Everyone else has their own gleaming road, too, but you can't see them."

My jaw drops and my open mouth instantly fills with water, so I have to roll over and float until the coughing stops. How incredibly embarrassing! What kind of swell-headed nincompoop thinks the moon shines only on her?!?

Well, this kind, apparently: the late-middle-aged, poetical, well-known-in-a-very-small-town kind. People usually grow out of this idea around age six, but some of us are late bloomers, and I imagine every adult still feels like the center of the universe once in a while.

We just hate to have to admit it.

Hating Summer

I don't mean to sound un-American or anything — especially this soon after the 4th of July — but it turns out that I hate summer. That's why I'm up at 5 a.m., just to get a little cool air so I can think straight. It's only 70 degrees outside, a civilized temperature, but it won't last long. By 8:30 it will be 80 and by 10 it will be 95 and then I'll begin hallucinating.

For someone like me, who defines herself by a certain amount of hustle and moxie, heat-induced lethargy is not just an overall drag, it's personality-shattering. By noon, the person I used to be — optimistic, cheerful, full of beans — will not remember her name, much less her plans for the day, none of which have been accomplished. The hot-weather me sloths around the house dropping things on the floor instead of putting them away. I take naps before noon, at noon, and after noon, and sometimes I go out in the yard and stand under the hose. In moments of concerted effort I'm able to find the paper's movie page and get myself to a matinee. This helps with the heat prostration, but not with getting any work done. And after you've seen Jersey Boys four times, there isn't much to glean from it — though I still love the music.

I don't hate everything about summer. Corn on the cob is good, eating real tomatoes. Swimming in the river. I like sleeping outside and watching the stars. It's just the darn heat — it unmans me, as the saying goes.

This is totally reasonable. First of all, I was born and raised in a fog bank on the north slope of San Francisco, where even on those rare days that the sun shone in July, there was always an ocean breeze. As Mark Twain is famous for possibly saying, "The coldest winter I ever spent was a summer in San Francisco." And second of all, my people are Scandinavians. There's a reason you do not find Scandinavians in the Summer Olympics. We are not truly comfortable without 25 lbs. of wool clothing and a hat on. When the temperature hits 68 in Oslo, pregnant women and the elderly are advised to stay indoors.

All reason aside, though, I am still faced with getting through summer. I pin my hair on top of

my head with an ice cube inside the bun. I limit
my wardrobe to white, off-white, and ivory. I walk
through the sprinklers. I drink water, iced tea,
lemonade, iced tea, and water. As the sweat beads
on my upper lip…and brow…and eyelids…and runs
down the back of my neck, and my skirt sticks to
the car seat, and I get third-degree burns from the
steering wheel, I try to remember that some of my
friends really love this weather, they wait all year for
it. They're out of their minds, of course, but it can't
be helped.

Their ancestors are not Scandinavians. I think
they're descended from rattlesnakes.

The Compost Pile

Now and then there's a topic I think of writing about, and my brain says, "No *way*!! That would *NOT* be a good idea, don't even think about it!" Maybe the subject is too politically sensitive or somehow in bad taste, but much of the time this reaction is because of how embarrassed I'd be to admit something. Coincidentally, this month I'm teaching an on-line class called "A Voice of Your Own — How to Write Intimately, Truthfully, and Fearlessly." Now I ask you, can the person who's teaching a class with this name really afford to worry about her own embarrassment? Of course not. *She* has to be brave and true and set an example, putting her pen and paper where her mouth is. *Ugh*. It's so annoying. Which leads me, reluctantly, to today's topic.

When I was a little girl, one of my brothers hated green peas, which at that time came in a frozen box you heated up in a pan of water on the stove. Every Thursday our family had chicken, rice, and peas, and my poor brother was faced with the dreaded green items again. What got him and the rest of us through this tense period in our lives was watching him learn to count and eat at the same time. I can't remember how many peas were required before he could leave the table, but my sister and I spent a lot of our suppertime listening to "nineteen, twenty, twenty-three, twenty-four..."

Cute story, huh? Now, almost half a century later, I'm the one who doesn't eat her vegetables. It isn't peas on a plate I'm resisting, though, it's my weekly share of fresh veggies from a local farm. Gorgeous heads of lettuce, dewy bok choi, carrots and zukes, all kinds of heirloom potatoes and many other delicacies are gathered up by rosy-cheeked interns and wait for me at the farm stand every Monday. I just dread this. I *want* to eat them all, I really do, but I can't. I roast some squash, make a little ratatouille with the eggplants, pesto from the fresh basil, and eat all the tomatoes. I take salads to every pot luck. On Sunday nights I stir fry whatever still looks reasonable from the fridge, where it's been lingering all week, so I have room in there to add the current week's new crop.

But sometimes, it just gets totally overwhelming. My students won't absorb one more offering of golden beets or lemon cucumbers and I have to resort to subterfuge. So here's what I do. *Promise* you won't tell anyone! I know I'll be run out of town. In the dead of night, I gather all the wilted, moldy, fragile, decomposing organic hand-picked vegetables from countertop and ice box bin and sneak them out to my compost pile. The whole world is asleep. I gingerly open the lid and fling them in.

I know this food should not go to waste, but I always think *this* week I'll be better. And then, once again, I'm not. It's horrible. It makes me feel so guilty that my stomach hurts.

Unless that sharp pain is from gulping down so many radishes last week.

Houston, We Have a Possum

Now some people, faced with a possum, would run screaming into the driveway. But I'm made of sterner stuff, and this was a small one: not a baby, possibly middle-school aged, and it wasn't moving. I'd looked down from the table where I was paying bills to a chair next to me, where the stamps were lying. Beside them, conjured out of thin air, was a small, silent, terrified-seeming animal staring at me.

I thought: "What the heck is that? Is that a possum?" Well, actually, my first thought was "eeeeeek!!!" But then I calmed down enough to wonder what it was and my brain registered "opossum." About a third the size of a cat, with a pointy nose. I took a brief walk around the living room. When I came back it was still there, so I bravely picked up the chair — stamps, possum, and all — carried it outside, and set it down on the patio. Then I ran into the house and slammed the door.

"Good grief!" I said aloud. "What is going on around here?!?" When I went to check half an hour later there was no possum so I brought the chair inside and put the stamps on my bills. "How weird," I thought. In 20 years of living in this town I've never seen a possum up close — a few killed on the road, and one trundling through a parking lot, but nothing this immediate. *Raccoons*, now, I've had *generations* of raccoons eating cat food in my kitchen at three in the morning. I know from raccoons, let me tell you. Great big raccoons full of vitamin- and mineral-rich hair-ball control formula cat food for seniors.

As I sat on the sofa a few weeks later, I heard some loud chewing, so loud I looked up from my book in amazement. Cats eating dry food will not make a racket. This sounded like someone was smashing individual pellets with a hammer. I dashed in there just in time to see the end of a thin tail whip around the side of the kitchen island. "Oh, no, a RAT???" I shrieked silently. Then its little valentine face peered around the corner. Possum. Same possum? Don't know. Bigger, and more bristly now, but still not full-grown.

"Ahem," I said, taking a step toward it. "This is not your house."

It shot like an arrow into the living room, making no sound, and instead of heading out the open front door like a sensible marsupial, scooted behind the sofa. Almost, I hate to say this, as if it were *familiar* with my sofa.

"This will not do," I said to all five cats, who were standing around watching. A few minutes went by, but nothing happened. Finally, I closed the front door, left the back one open, hid the cat food, and went to bed out on my deck. I have no idea what happened to the possum. But you know there's only one way stories like this end, right?

With those three dreaded words: "To be continued…"

Nowhere to Hide

People are doing a lot of moving around lately
— and I don't mean zumba class, I mean relocating.
A poet friend just shipped her little family back to
their home state of Michigan from Silicon Valley,
prompted by a job change. One of my youngest
friends stopped cutting hair in Denver and now
walks dogs in Portland. That's Portland, Oregon, for
any of you not on the West Coast. There's only one
Portland out here.

Much has been written over the years about
the peripatetic American lifestyle and how much
it's changed since World War II. This feels different
to me. People are wondering which places will be
safest from the growing effects of climate change.
One young couple is looking at land near Homer,
Alaska right now: good when the temperature rises,
not great when sea levels do. Others have checked
out rural Maine, Vermont's Northeast Kingdom,

western Washington State, and Minnesota. Not to mention those leaving L.A. and San Francisco to move into my neighborhood: the Sierra foothills.

It's fascinating to watch. When I unpacked here twenty years ago, I thought Nevada County might well be my last location. I came for love, not a change of scene, but once I'd arrived, I liked the arts-rich small-town feel of the place and its relative distance from civilization. This was the right size pond for the kind of fish I was turning out to be. Plus, Gary Snyder lived here. In the world of poets, that's like moving onto the same street as God.

At 2500 feet, we're not concerned with sea-level...nor hurricanes, tornados, or tsunamis. What we think about, morning, noon, and night, is fire.

A friend reminds me the planet's not going to fall apart at one exact moment, which is what my brain seems to fear. Disasters will occur like popcorn heating in a skillet. Separate isolated events, slowly at first, with refugees escaping the affected area, as they've done in boats from Syria to Greece and in cars from Fort McMurray to Edmonton. Over time, it will speed up: things will happen so fast that helping people in place or accommodating refugees is going to become more difficult. There isn't really anywhere to go that doesn't have some tendency to get overwhelming, whether by drought, flooding, earthquakes, unquenchable fires, or war.

Part of the current restlessness is practical: a businesswoman watches insurance rates go through the roof and then become unavailable as the big carriers stop insuring against fire in California. In a few years her options will be to close down or to move. And I completely understand people leaving urban traffic jams and high rents.

But some of this wanderlust seems fueled by agitation. We don't know what's coming, how it will unfold, or when. This is really not fun for humans. Maybe it won't be as bad, we think, if we go somewhere else.

How about you? Are you having a big yard sale this weekend? Are your suitcases by the door already? What's your plan?

Because August

Here we are at the time of year when, if you like to put up food for the winter, you really start to feel overwhelmed. For some reason every single tomato on every vine in the county has to get ripe at the same time. Whose nutty idea was that? It's all or nothing, a kind of polarized thinking that humans have been training themselves out of for decades. But are the vegetables listening? They are not. They don't care about us and our busy lives. It's very sad.

And it's not just tomatoes. Everything else is bursting and ready to pick too: melons and cucumbers, 42 kinds of summer squashes, plums, peaches, mild and hot peppers, corn, more corn, green beans, onions, garlic, kale, potatoes…oh, my Lord, the basil! The urgency of it all is both thrilling and terrifying, especially if you're hoping to save some of this plenty to eat during the winter. You have about ten days before all of it begins to soften

and fall to the ground or, in the case of zucchini,
secretly grow to the size of a birchbark canoe while
you're not looking.

Having a vegetable garden seems both morally
right and straightforward: you plant in the spring,
you weed and do a little watering in the summer,
you harvest in fall and end up with satisfying rows
of jars on your kitchen shelves. Sometimes you
get to wear a cute floppy hat. The backyard smells
glorious. Nobody mentions those disgusting tomato
cut-worms that are the size of your cell-phone, or
the fact that every single thing you plant is going
to need your attention at exactly the same moment.
Talk about pressure! It's insane.

There's a joke that says in August people all
over the Midwest lock their car doors, while the rest
of the time they don't bother. As my brain tries to
make sense of this, thinking: "Do they Christmas
shop that early, and don't want the presents stolen?"
the punchline unspools from my memory banks. Oh,
yeah. It's not about theft, it's about generosity. The
doors are locked so your neighbors don't sneak in
and leave you bags of enormous unsightly zucchini.

I once ended up at a County Fair on Salt Spring
Island, in Washington State, where someone had
built a wonderful ski-jump-like contraption on

which to race vegetables. I laughed till tears ran down my cheeks to see four little plastic wheels stabbed into the underside of a two-foot-long zucchini and its handy win over a glossy Asian eggplant. This seemed like an excellent use for extra vegetables: entertainment for island-bound people facing another winter.

But back to the tomatoes. To paraphrase Elisabeth Kubler-Ross, there are five stages of August: Denial, Anger, Bargaining, Depression, and Canning. Even though it's 102 in the shade, my hot water bath is steaming. The jars are clean, the lids are sterile, the tomatoes have been skinned and chopped. Are you ready? Good luck!

On your mark, get set…. GO!!!

Piles of Tomatoes on the Highway

Driving to the coast this week I saw three Teslas, two Jaguars, and one double tractor-trailer full of tomatoes, which were rounded on top and uncovered. If you don't live in tomato country, you won't have seen random piles of them at freeway exits the way we have. These come from the trucks tilting a bit when they head into the curve of the exit too fast and the top 30 or 40 fruits sliding off. It took me a while to figure it out when I first moved inland, but once I saw the process with my own eyes it made sense. Before that I was inventing stories about how they got there: that they were altars to the God of Vegetables-That-Are-Really-Fruits, or an inventive method to lure herds of deer off the freeways — not plausible in the least, but kind of fun. This is what writers do when we drive.

Two of the Teslas were white and one was gray, both Jaguars were cherry red and vintage: the saloon car type. No, it was not the same vehicle seen twice. All of them sped past me. If there'd been any dust on the freeway I would have been left in it, but there wasn't. This is part of my new longevity plan: next week I won't just be 60, I will be 61, which is officially "in my sixties" and a whole different ball of wax. Extreme measures must be taken. So I've decided to really and truly stay no more than five miles over the posted speed.

I do have some good habits: I never pass on the right, nor linger in the fast lane, which completely screws up the flow of traffic. I don't use my phone in the car for any reason, since Maggie McKaig caught me once at a local stop sign and wrote me a concerned, kind, tough love e-mail about it three years ago. I calculate that she's saved my life at least 12 times now by doing so, and I'm very grateful. Sometimes we need a little shove in the right direction, even those of us who like to think we're already perfect and prefer to perform the shoving rather than receive it.

My sister has blue tooth and whatnot, so she makes all her calls legally from the car. I stopped twice at pull-outs to talk to her. I also stopped, sequentially, to buy fresh cherries, gas, and an iced tea, and once I got within a few miles of my destination, to stretch my legs and smell the air.

On our coast here, in Northern California, the
fog usually rolls out to sea some time in the morning
and the sun warms everything up, braiding the scents
of ocean salt, roadside fennel, and eucalyptus into
a pungent rope many of us can follow straight back
to childhood. Back to a picnic table at Point Lobos
or Stinson Beach, where our feet didn't reach the
ground and we ate tomato sandwiches on white bread
with mayonnaise for lunch and couldn't imagine
being older than 18, much less as ancient as 61.

The Width of Nevada

Yesterday I drove the width of Nevada, east to west, in a black Toyota with my friend Julia. We were on Highway 50, which lived up to its name as the Loneliest Road in America — we saw only a handful of other vehicles over the course of a whole day. This was fine with me. My brain gets overfull in my daily life and appreciates hour after hour of long vistas with nothing but sage to look at.

I love the way Nevada isn't flat. Between ranges of mountains, the land slopes down into huge shallow valleys and then slopes up again. You can see the road ahead of you for about 70 miles. Every now and then a stand of trees indicates some habitation, maybe thriving, maybe abandoned.

We saw cattle, but not many. A beautiful black hawk with a white patch above his tail. Once in a while many little gray birds would scatter up from the highway in front of us just in the nick of time.

I couldn't figure out what they might be trying to eat off the asphalt. The only coyotes we saw were roadkill, but there were mule deer bounding away, and one long-eared jack rabbit. Three or four puffy clouds. We were returning from hiking in Southern Utah, a dramatically beautiful place, and almost as empty as Nevada.

I always forget, until I leave home, how hugely important it is for writers to look at different landscapes, whether it's rainy side-streets in Paris or sandy trails through the Grand Staircase-Escalante National Monument. It rearranges our thinking in wonderful ways. A new vocabulary appears: I kept hearing my mouth speak words I don't normally use: canyon and thunderhead. Rimrock. Granary. Pictograph. My lips and teeth made their way around Anasazi and Pueblo. I tasted chiles and combinations of spices I'd never tried before, got used to walking four thousand feet higher than my own neighborhood.

The benefits of this kind of adventure aren't limited to writers. An oncologist I know says that travel is the best thing anyone can do for her immune system. It wakes up your cells from their routines and this alertness makes them stronger and better able to defend against invasion. The change in air and food — in sensory input of all kinds, even in language — requires us to adapt, to stretch and get a little more flexible all over.

I know travel is heart-expanding: it helps me understand other people's lives and perspectives. I look more closely at everything because it's unfamiliar, which gets me back into the groove of noticing and describing what I *actually* see, instead of generalizing and making assumptions, the bane of good writing.

When we got to the outskirts of Reno and the sensory assault of traffic and casinos, I still felt calm, and open-hearted. If you can let a Dodge Ram cut you off and not even feel your blood pressure rise, you know you've had a real vacation.

Giftiness

I think of myself as a capable person —
competent, diligent, of at least average bravery. I'm
always bustling around, hauling myself up by my
bootstraps rather than thinking anyone's going to
come along and save me. Consequently, I'm not that
accustomed to receiving help.

But last week one of my friends, a new-ish
friend, overheard me talking about a task I was
preparing to do and with a big smile whisked it
right out of my hands. This was business-related:
she used her business to help my business. She
did it faster and far more elegantly than I would
have been able to, and it was a gift. I felt a little
dizzy. Something I had been slightly dreading was
suddenly not just handled, but gorgeous, a thing to
admire and show off.

Mixed in among my feelings of gratitude and
wonder was confusion. Is this allowed? Aren't

I supposed to be doing everything myself? Do I deserve this? I have to say, as well as really great, it felt the tiniest bit scary.

Isn't this sad? In our world, which is based so firmly on exchanges of equal value usually involving money, we aren't used to receiving gifts. Most of us are a little suspicious, particularly if they're large gifts from someone outside the family, and it isn't our birthday.

Lewis Hyde wrote a wonderful book called *The Gift*, in which he talks about an underground economy of gift-giving that exists behind our monetary, day-to-day economy. Certain indigenous groups measure status not by how much they acquire, but by how much they can give away. Some Pacific Northwest Indian tribes ceremonially gave salmon bones back to the river after they'd caught the fish and eaten the meat. Hyde places poetry within the gift economy because it has almost no financial value in the other one. How much would you pay for a single poem? You might buy a book of them, but it's equally likely a friend would send you a poem that moved her and you'd pass it to your mother, who'd put it on her ice box. From this angle, my entire career is based on giving.

Even though I'm not used to receiving, I do believe in balance. My friends are nice enough to take what I give them without getting nuts about it, and it seems only right that I should afford them the same opportunity. It just may be a little while before I can do it gracefully.

When this friend printed 450 letterpress bookmarks with silver ink on chocolate-colored paper, she saved me a ton of work. It took her two hours. She already had the ink and the paper. She prints things all day long. It was easy for her, in the way writing is easy for me.

When I thanked her for the 83rd time, she said she liked doing things for me because she could see how much I appreciated them. And she's right about that. I'm grateful down to my toes.

In honor of her, and to encourage us all to do things we aren't good at yet, I might even write an essay about it.

Possum 1, Poet 0

Just when I was thinking I might make it through summer with no wild animal encounters, another possum has shown up in my kitchen. I say "another," because we had one last year who came around for about a month to steal cat food. On arrival it was a very small example of its kind, but it grew to the size of a 1963 Volkswagen bus, nourished by expensive grain-free cat food, melon rinds from the compost, and ticks.

Did you know possums eat ticks? Thousands of ticks a year. This is their great social benefit, besides being the only marsupial north of Mexico and so a convenient subject for middle school science reports.

Possums start out the size of your thumb, spend a couple of months hanging off the backs of their mothers, and then show up next to the cat food bowl when they're about 10 weeks old and very, very cute. This cute stage is fleeting. It lasts just long

enough to lure you into curiosity and fascination, by
which time the possum has scoped out your house,
established a detente with your cats, and found the
best place in the yard to sleep all day undisturbed.
When sleeping, in case you forgot that science report
you wrote in middle school, possums hang upside
down by their tails in trees, kind of like hairy gray
Christmas ornaments.

If I go to bed at 9:00, I am likely to miss all the
action. Sometimes this is a good thing. If I stay
up till 11:00, though, I will likely see the possum
waddle in my open back door, pass the desk where
I'm calmly sitting since by now I've learned not to
shriek, and approach the cat food.

When my cats eat, they face the wall and
chew quietly. Their species has pretended to be
domesticated for 9000 years. The possum, however,
is wild, and squeezes him or herself between
the bowl and the wall to face out, where danger
might come from — or an irritable poet. Quiet
is not involved: he or she makes a huge racket
with every bite. Possums have a long snout and
jaw, with many pointy little teeth, kind of like a
shark. Ticks, as you'll remember, are very hard to
squish so it makes sense that a possum is good at
crunching things. The sound would be perfect in a

Lord of the Rings sequel to convey a dragon eating bones.

Last year's possum took refuge under my sofa when it was scared, rather than going back outside the clearly visible open doors. Somehow, through DNA or marsupial folklore, this habit has been passed down to the new possum, who zips under the furniture's pleated hem and then sticks his nose back out again to sniff what I'm doing.

You know what I'm doing, of course. I'm standing there, hands on hips, saying, "This is ridiculous! Don't you dare have any babies under my sofa!!" and wondering what will happen next.

SPENDING DAYLIGHT

Ready for Anything?

There are two kinds of people in the world, my brother Sam and I used to joke: the kind who do this and the kind who don't. The kind who reach across the seat to open the car door for you, and the kind who don't. The kind who put cash in a tip jar and the kind who don't. Sam once got so mad at me he blurted out "There are two kinds of people in this world, Molly, and *you are not* one of them!!" That's made us laugh ever since, and is a good ice breaker during tense conversations, like the one about keeping an emergency bag beside your front door in case of fire or earthquake.

I'm the kind of person who talks about a go-bag but isn't great at compiling it. I have one, I do. In it, there's a list of important phone numbers, and a can opener. I rotate prescription med bottles to it each month after I decant the pills into something else. I have unsalted cashews, good through 2017, and a mini flashlight but no extra batteries. Three cans of cat food, a map of evacuation routes, my passport. Kitchen matches in a zip-lock bag. One pair of socks. Two pens and a pad of paper. A teensy drugstore first aid kit that doesn't even contain aspirin.

No water. No radio. No money. The cashews will last a day and we're told to have provisions for three at least, and better yet: two weeks. I don't have a bag in the car, should a fire take out my neighborhood while I'm at work and require me to flee from elsewhere.

Probably the same principle operates in humans about disaster planning as it does about death. Somewhere in our deepest secret heart of hearts, we can't believe it will happen to us. This principle is why people marry more than twice, and still buy homes in Florida with a straight face.

As climate change begins to — oh, what a coincidence! — actually change the climate, we're all being put on notice that something is likely, fairly soon but we're not sure how or when, to happen to us. It's kind of a cool time to be alive. Feeling my own brain get used to this, and watching the behavior of everyone around me is fascinating.

Last week people I know evacuated due to a nearby fire, so things got very real. They had time

to run around videotaping the living room and
deciding what not to leave behind. People, animals,
photographs was what I kept hearing. Almost
nothing else was worth taking. (The question arises,
then why do we have all this stuff?)

One of my friends has a complete go-bag, and
has practiced! She's strapped it and the cat carrier
to her bike and ridden the three miles to her local
evacuation center. The only thing she didn't bring
on this trial run was the cat. I'm buying batteries
and a camping water purifier today, and more
cashews.

There are two kinds of people in the world, it
turns out: the ones who are actually prepared and
the ones who aren't.

Give Me a Break

Even though I'm nearly perfect in all ways, there are a few minor character flaws that surface once in a while. In particular, I wrestle with the strangely compelling idea that I deserve some sort of break. I don't know if this is because I'm white, or American, or was raised upper-middle class or all of the above, but it comes over me quickly and with great force. This often happens when there's some task ahead of me I would prefer not to do, like stacking firewood or weeding.

The antidote to entitlement is gratitude, but when I feel put-upon, possibly even a teensy bit *resentful*, as I did today, I forget all about being grateful. My inner victim is sure everyone owes her something and she shouldn't have to be bothered. And she's hard to reason with. If you're a parent, you've dealt with this thousands of times. I find what works on me is a kind of calm hyper-adult persistent logic when I feel a tantrum building,

    First I let my whiney victimized self say what she thinks, and then I find something to counter with. *I hate stacking firewood!* But isn't it great to be warm in winter? *I don't want to take out the trash.* I love how someone picks it up and we don't have to drive to the dump. *I don't want to make dinner!* These fresh eggs are delicious. *I hate eggs!* You eat eggs all the time! *I'm not doing the dishes tonight, I'm too tired.* That's okay, you can do them in the morning. *Nobody loves me!* You have an awful lot of friends for someone nobody loves. *If anyone loved me they'd come stack this darn firewood!* Are you ready to go to their house and stack theirs? *Oh, shut UP!!!*

    At a certain point, my inner victim starts crying in frustration, which clears the air, or sees how absurd her remarks are and begins to laugh. Either way, the spell is broken. It helps to remember that I feel victimized when faced with expectations: my own or somebody else's. Today, I think I was channeling my grandmother, who stacked her firewood quickly so it wasn't an eyesore in the driveway.

    My grandmother's been gone for 22 years, and I don't really care what people think of a big pile of logs in *my* driveway. The renter who has to back around them hasn't complained. I work for a living and my grandmother did not — she had more time to stack wood, and came from a tidy generation, very concerned about what the neighbors thought. She also had grandchildren to do some of her work for her.

After I figured this out, I felt much less crabby. My inner victim retired to the depths of my psyche, grumbling, to await further injustices, and I put on some work gloves and went outside.

Don't tell anyone, but I actually like stacking wood.

Spending Daylight

When I was a kid, my favorite day of the year was, predictably, Christmas, followed closely by my birthday. Now that I'm old enough to know Santa Claus is a folktale and I've had so many birthdays that they loom as very mixed blessings, my favorite day of the year is today. Not today as in "oh, wow, groovy, man, be here now." But today, the day we turn the clocks back and stop saving daylight.

When I wake up in the morning to that extra hour, I feel as rich as Bill & Melinda Gates. My whole body relaxes more deeply. I lie in bed and watch sunshine come through the living room windows and hit a mirror, whose beveled edges reflect at an angle, so lovely patterns of light appear as if by magic on my bedroom wall. Having the sun come up again so early throws my nervous system back into mid-summer. Even though the wood stove is warm and there's frost on my office roof, I'm awash in early-August optimism.

This benevolent feeling usually lasts a few days — it follows me as I move from clock to clock changing the time since I forgot to last night. I have enormous energy to do boring things like transport the summer clothes up to the garage and haul the winter clothes down. I even lifted the air conditioner out of my office window and carried it up to its storage spot all by myself, a Herculean feat.

Then I sat on the floor for a while and watched my cats as they all slept on the same piece of furniture, something they haven't done since last winter. Their legs and tails were tangled in a big confusion, and, as usual, India was resting his cheek against one of Sprocket's ears, so he looked a little squashed. Sid lay on his back with three of his four huge feet in the air — he and Gracie are polydactyl, with seven toes on each foot. One front leg extended over his head as though he were practicing a yoga move, not quite grazing Gracie's back where she lay curled into the smallest ball imaginable.

These cats are used to me being a sap. I talk to them all the time, mostly in English, but sometimes in Norwegian, telling them how wonderful they are, and how much mackerel they surely deserve if

only I had a fishing pole. I read them my new poems
while they sleep. I patiently clean up the entrails
of the gophers they devour on the living room floor,
and the disgusting little jawbones. After they have
thoroughly cleaned their coats of burrs and spit
them all over my blankets, I shake the blankets
without complaint.

As the days get shorter and shorter and we
gradually *spend* this precious hour of light we gained
today, my mood will begin to slide inexorably into the
basement. But the cats always remind me, in their
throaty version of Norwegian, that I am an animal
too, and hibernation is nothing to be afraid of.

A Dark Night in the Daytime

I'm not sure what's come over me lately, but I feel very divided...as though part of me is perfectly happy to continue on whatever path I seem to be on: teaching poetry, canning pears, eating dinner with friends. But another part is standing still, looking around, saying "Why would anyone keep doing all these things? What does it matter? Does anything matter? Who the heck am I, anyway?"

I'd call this a "dark night of the soul," as Saint John of the Cross, the Spanish poet and Roman Catholic mystic did, except it's 11 in the morning and I don't know what souls actually are. It does feel dark, though, whatever it is.

Let me say that I'm not suicidal. I don't feel suicidal at all. This is almost worse: a stoppage of everything right in its tracks. I've felt suicidal a few times in my life, and that seems to have energy in it, a kind of push to avoid pain, which is why it's something to worry about. The energy might lead to action.

This isn't avoidance. It feels more like standing still and letting the pain hit you full force. There's nowhere to go. At the same time, however, one of my cats is barfing in the living room and there's laundry in the washing machine that needs to go in the dryer. I haven't made my teaching plan for this afternoon's class, and have nothing in the house for lunch.

I expect, if I did even a tiny amount of research, I could find many volumes describing this feeling. From Thomas More to Eckhart Tolle. From Anne Sexton to Mary Oliver and millions of places in between, others have tried to make sense of it. But I'm stuck here, unable to crack open a book, or punch the word "Wikipedia" into my cell phone. My arms don't want to move. My brain is sure I'm the only person who's ever felt this bereft and alone.

It might be the holidays looming that brought this on. What with my not-fun memories of childhood and lack of a personal nuclear family, the Thanksgiving-Christmas-New Year's trifecta always feels remote, no matter how hard I try to engage myself singing carols, making presents, and admiring the twinkly lights. It might be because

I'm looking closely at giving up one of my long-time companions, sugar. Maybe Pluto is in my House of Mirth, and went retrograde.

I'm a sucker for reasons. If you can figure out a reason, then you can explain to yourself what's going on, which is — for some of us — soothing. But I'm not sure there's a reason here, or rather, there are so many it's impossible to choose.

If there *is* a God, perhaps he or she rotates the human burden of grief and this is my month to help carry it. Or maybe a coral-pink tree frog deep in the Amazon just went extinct, and I'm the person assigned to mourn.

Now That I'm Fat

Lately I've been asking myself questions that begin with "What if?" I just got tired of framing my thoughts to myself using the verb "should," as in: *You really should put the wet laundry that's been in the machine for three days into the dryer*. Hearing "should" makes me react immediately with *No way! I'm busy! Don't tell ME what to do!* Eventually I work around to doing whatever it is, but it might take some time, and meanwhile the wet laundry has molded.

So I decided to see if open-ended questions instead of judgement would have a different effect, and the change has been a rousing success. Asking a question prompts my mind to ditch the attitude and come up with answers: *What if you dried that three-day old wet laundry?* leads me to: *Well, let's see, it wouldn't mold, and I could wear my black pants tonight, and I like folding laundry,* and so forth. My heart fills with possibility instead of resistance, and life rolls along much more smoothly.

Some learned person once said that what you resist persists. Often when I hear this phrase, I'm so beguiled by how similar *resist* and *persist* sound that I ignore the larger meaning — a poet's type of distraction. But today I'm thinking about the meaning, and looking at my resistances. They are numerous, but there are two at the top of the list that outweigh (you should pardon the phrase) all the rest: being fat, and being single. The way I resist being fat is to not accept it: I don't want to be fat, and I didn't used to be fat, and I don't want anyone to think I'm fat. I sashay around as if I'm not fat, and the whole production is a great big sham because whenever I look at myself in a mirror I'm horrified at my size.

What if, instead, I started to state the truth once in a while? Just as an experiment. Here, I'll try it with you. *I'm fat. Everyone who sees me knows that I'm fat. I didn't used to be fat, it's true, but I am now. No matter how beautifully I dress, how graceful my carriage, and how sweet my smile, no matter how good my poems are, I'm fat. F-A-T, fat.*

The first thing that pops into my mind is "so?" That is not what I usually hear. I usually hear: you shouldn't be fat, it's not good to be fat, people won't like you if you're fat, men won't be attracted to you, you'll always be single, you'll die young, you clearly don't have any self-control, fat is disgusting, you should be ashamed of yourself.

Aha. *You should be ashamed of yourself.* You know what? That is a total crock. I may be fat, and I may be single, and I may earn less money than your average busboy, but one thing I am NOT is ashamed of myself. All I do all day long is try to be as kind and compassionate and productive and creative and truthful as I know how. These are not things to be ashamed of. These are things to celebrate!

If what we resist persists, then it figures that what we accept dissipates, right? I'll let you know if I lose any weight, now that I'm fat.

Deadwood

For the first time since I was in high school, I have fallen in love with a television show. We can blame this on my friend Marilyn. She knows I'm writing a book of poems about a pioneer family, and she kept telling me that Deadwood, on HBO, would be great background for the book.

I have been living quite happily without TV reception for almost five years now, reading a lot of novels. But recently a neighbor put in one of those baby satellite dishes, and the guy who came to install it was very persuasive. So now I'm linked to the little gray cupped ear on my neighbor's porch railing, and thus to one of those pseudo-stars spinning overhead.

Marilyn told me that Deadwood — a show about a mining town in 1877 South Dakota — was full of amazingly bad language, and she was right. Every third word is something I wouldn't say in front of my niece. It's a two-part word, the first half a synonym for rooster, and the second a synonym for lollipop. You get the idea.

At first I was kind of appalled. Having been raised on Laura Ingalls Wilder, and then The Magnificent Seven, I was used to a certain tone. Even Louis L'Amour, that writer of thinly disguised romance novels for men about the West, never put more than "tarnation!" into his villains' mouths, and usually they just scowled and spat on the floor.

In Deadwood, between exclamations of "rooster-lollipop," someone is always getting shot or knifed or beaten to death and then fed to the Chinaman's pigs. I don't know if I'm more disturbed by the routine and casual slaughter or by the news that pigs eat human flesh, which is certainly going to change my approach to the County Fair. Compared to this, the language seems almost benign. And that's part of the point.

Deadwood's creator, David Milch, argues pretty convincingly that in this violent, lawless setting, saying "rooster-lollipop" is a safety valve, a way to express anger without having to use your Derringer. I'm not sure I believe this, but I do know that when I'm furious, stomping around the house and swearing helps me feel better. I don't usually do it in front of the person I'm mad at, but maybe that's where 130 years of progress has brought us.

There's something very satisfying about all those harsh one-syllable Anglo-Saxon words ending in consonants. They're tailor-made to spit out. They sound just like an axe hitting a tree. Try it with "truck" and "blunt." Can't you hear the blade sink in?

I'm not sure how Deadwood will end up influencing my pioneer poems — it's great to see the wagons and clothes and how dusty everything is. But my people are farming and raising goats rather than mining, running whorehouses, and downing shots of whiskey every ten minutes. There just isn't much reason to call anyone "rooster-lollipop."

But I'll see if somehow I can work it in.

More Than Your John Hancock

Yesterday, I paid my bills. I took them to a café, sat at the counter and wrote twelve checks. Stuck on return-address labels, slapped on some colorful Latin Music stamps and put the envelopes in size order. Then I stopped by the P.O. on the way home to drop them into the outside box.

I know this is old-fashioned of me, but I love writing my checks. I put "exactly" before a round amount like forty dollars, the way my mother did. My dates read "23 October, 2016." I love the idea that humans have carried paper letters from sender to recipient for centuries. It makes me feel part of a long chain of humanity that includes the Pony Express riders. Call me nostalgic and sentimental, I don't care.

Many of my friends pay automatically, through their computers. I can see the benefits: efficiency, track-ability, less paper in the recycling bin. But

there's one huge downside: no handwriting.
Look around your own life. When do you write
by hand any more? Parents make lists with their
smartphone's note function. VPs write dates in iCal
using their thumbs. Postcards are vanishing from
the 21st century landscape and letters are pretty
much already gone. These days most people just
write their names…on credit card signature lines or
at the voting booth. Maybe on a birthday card. When
was the last time you wrote a complete sentence by
hand?

The trouble with progress is that after a while
there are a lot of people in the world who don't
understand what they're missing. Good things get
lost, and then the people who knew about them
grow old and the last, say, roadside telephone booth
disappears.

My grandmother, born in 1906, began writing
letters to me when I was seven and I still have most
of them. She wrote in green ball point and signed
them with a little drawing of a seagull. Her writing
was legible but you could tell she was thinking fast.
She had a rushing-around personality that her
handwriting reflected: sharp pointy letters, and
lots of width as the pen raced across the page. Not
big round grade-school printing like my Mom's,

which I admired but could never replicate. The word "signature" isn't metaphoric: both of them expressed character traits through their writing, in a way that choosing among ten fonts and using emoticons on a screen just can't compete with. My mom was patient and followed most of the rules. My grandmother was in a hurry to get outside and live her real life, banding birds.

I'm aware that handwriting, like the phone booth, is doomed. But just like my crusades on behalf of proper grammar and using the word "bottom" instead of that synonym for a donkey when you're speaking in public, it will disappear over my dead body, and I mean that literally.

Do me a favor and write something by hand today, just to prove you haven't forgotten how. Please? For me? A song lyric, a to-do list. A homemade prayer.

The Color of My Car

When I was little, apparently I wouldn't leave
the house unless my socks were folded over exactly
in half. My mother related this with humor, but
you could see the exasperation in her eyes, too, as
she remembered those days of dressing my sister
and me before she took us anywhere. This was the
mid-fifties, when you didn't go on airplanes without
wearing your Sunday best. Even a grocery store trip
required lipstick. With two kids under one-and-a-
half, she must have gone bananas on a regular basis
just stuffing us into clean clothes, much less having
one of us fuss over fashion details like sock height.

Families pass on these apocryphal stories
to explain the character of their members, and
while I don't fold my socks over any more, I have
other, similar demands about beauty and order.
For instance, I care about the color of my car. I've
probably incited a collective groan from all the men

within earshot, and I don't fault you for it. But I can't help it. I know the drive-train is important, the state of the tires, the fluid levels. I wasn't born yesterday. It's just that listening to a purring engine doesn't warm the cockles of my heart the way admiring a nice paint job does, when it's the right color.

I mention this because I'm looking for a new car. A new used car, that is. I've never bought a new car in my life, because at the moment when I drove across that little invisible line between the car lot and the street, that line where the car's value goes down by several thousand dollars in half a second, all my grandparents would have heart attacks right on the spot. They're already dead, but they'd still have heart attacks. They lived through the Depression, and no argument could make them think it was reasonable to lose that kind of money voluntarily.

So I'm looking for a used car, and I'd like it to be exactly like my current car, which is a maroon Toyota Rav4. As far as I can tell from looking on the internet, there are eight Rav4's for sale in the United States in my price range. Most of them are in North Carolina, which is not where I live. None of them are maroon.

I can see my next few weeks are going to be full of compromises. This is what happens in life. Cars, jobs, boyfriends, you name it. You start out looking for a dark-colored late-'90s Rav4 with fewer than a hundred thousand miles on it, and you end up buying a white Mazda Protegé with one blue fender, or a late-'80s Jetta that's only been in two collisions. I guess I'd better prepare myself.

Although, who knows? Maybe a miracle will happen and I'll find exactly what I want. I'm thinking of folding my socks precisely in half while I'm searching.

In honor of my thrifty grandparents, and because it's got to be good luck.

Trimming Season

It's been a quiet week in Nevada City, my home town…School has begun, so the traffic jams are concentrated again around 8:00 and 3:00, and the municipal swimming pool is empty. Those hundreds of locals who went to Burning Man and left all the good parking spaces open have come back and filled them again. The seasonal migrant workers who descend on us annually to trim newly-harvested marijuana are starting to arrive, sleeping in their cars in out of the way places and smelling forcibly of skunk. It's a typical autumn in Northern California.

Last year, the word "trimmigrant" suddenly appeared, an amalgam of "trimmer" and "immigrant" that sounds a bit derogatory. I prefer "trimmer," though this might be confusing to someone who sews or frequents the beauty parlor. Taking swipes with a razor to subdue your pubic foliage is also called "trimming," and the word's been common for centuries when you're decorating curtains.

This kind of trimmer, the marijuana kind, is more often a middle class white kid from Ann Arbor or Ames than a Spanish-speaker with experience in artichoke fields. And a certain entitlement can come with that background. The wave of people entering our fairly small gold-mining tourist town are known for not following local laws and taking advantage of things we do for our homeless population, like offer free meals from local restaurants called Gratitude Bowls.

This year someone, I don't know who, distributed a flyer called "Etiquette Primer, for Trimmigrants and Those Who Employ Them," which is full of useful suggestions. Along with links to bus schedules, campgrounds, and local M.D.s, it lists regulations about smoking inside city limits, loitering laws, trespassing, and the fines for all of these. It warns of extreme local fire danger, recommends where to walk your dog, and updates us all on the fact that trimmers can be arrested for felony cultivation if they don't have a valid California doctor's recommendation to use medical marijuana.

Something about this makes me howl with laughter. In this county, we live at the crossroads of idealism and reality. There are two competing ideals, though: one that pot doesn't exist and the other that pot is legal, available, beneficial, and normal. The reality is, of course, in between: pot is illegal, but it's also our cash crop, some of the best in the world, and the reason many businesses are still open and many tourists flock here. Even though quite a few of our public officials don't seem to believe this: it's the purring Tesla engine of our local economy.

Ideally, we'd have no migrant labor force sitting on sidewalks blocking traffic and scaring ordinary visitors away from hat shops and wine bars. But since we do, I think it's a great idea to admit it, and brilliant to hand out tips on how things work here, and how we'd like trimmers to behave.

Whether they follow these suggestions is another matter entirely. It's between them and their own consciences if they make $200 a day tax-free and then take advantage of a Gratitude Bowl.

On Not Becoming a Ballerina

Well, I seem to be having a mid-life crisis. I hoped to avoid this by staying very busy in the middle of my life, which was around age 37. Even though many Baby Boomers pretend middle age begins at 75 and old age doesn't really start until a few days after you've died, some of us have enough common sense to remember that two plus two equals four, or in this case, 37 plus 37 equals 74. Seventy-four sounds young the closer we get to it but is in fact a reasonable lifespan, and longer than both my parents lived. I'm frankly a little surprised I made it to 60, and perhaps that's part of the problem.

Do you remember the day you realized you weren't ever going to be a ballerina? This strikes a girl at about 15. Real ballerinas start dance classes when they're six or seven and continue in a somewhat driven and fanatical manner for a

decade, appearing in the Nutcracker each of those
years. They wear their hair slicked back in a bun
and walk with their toes turned out like ducks down
the halls of American grade schools, middle schools,
and high schools. They're also, pretty clearly from
the age of six, built like gazelles: long of leg, narrow
of hip, small of bosom. The rest of us, built like
an assortment of other African animals, carry on
happily ignoring pliés and at some point realize
it's too late: we aren't going to be able to catch up.
Our 15-year-old bones are too old to slip easily into
fourth position, and American Ballet Theater is now
out of reach.

It's interesting facing this sort of loss at 15.
It's both shocking — because it's real — and silly
— because most of us didn't want to be ballerinas
in the first place, and we're so young almost every
other option is still open to us. But I bet if you
interviewed ten random women on the street and
asked when they knew they weren't going to be a
ballerina, each would have an answer for you. I'm
not sure if there's a parallel situation for boys —
perhaps Major League relief pitcher.

I did not turn out to be a ballerina. I'm also not
a mother, and lately, now my friends' kids are having
babies, I'm aware I'm not a grandmother, either.

This doesn't really bother me...much...but it opens the door to the question, "Well what the heck am I, then?" A very cold draft is blowing through that door.

I've been a waitress, house-cleaner, sweater designer, bookkeeper, Fortune 1000 lender, investigator for the EEOC. A poet, a teacher, a speaker, a radio commentator, a painter, a radical life coach. Also a daughter, sister, niece, aunt, cousin, girlfriend, fiancee, and landlady. I've been a bridesmaid, a cocaine addict, a rower. I've written six books and sung Beethoven's Missa Solemnis in Boston's Symphony Hall.

My question is, who cares? What does any of this matter? And what am I supposed to do now? If you think of an answer, please drop me an e-mail, before I tear out all of my nearly completely gray hairs.

Normal Every-Day Sloth & Torpor

Last night I was talking to some friends about cooking. Both of these women raised children, so you know they put a lot of food on the table over the years, whether they felt like it or not.

I have not had children, nor have I spent long years living with and feeding another adult. Every time I get into a new romantic relationship I'm shocked all over again at how often dinner comes around, and the expectation that as a woman I might somehow be responsible for satisfying any one else's hunger. It's not that I don't like cooking — I do. But I go through phases, and right now reservations are what I make best, or a quick phone order from the local pizza joint to be picked up on my way home from work. I tested this again last week, inviting a new friend over, and lasted until 4 p.m. before I caved and had to suggest we go out instead. I *wanted* to want to make dinner for her, but I just couldn't manage to start the prep in time. It all seemed way too exhausting.

Does this happen to you? Do some of those do-it-every-day-or-week jobs like cooking, cleaning, laundry, flossing your teeth, getting your oil changed, and mowing the lawn suddenly turn into Mt. Everest without warning? I am wondering if this is normal, or whether I'm having another mid-life crisis.

It's not just cooking. Lately I've been doing laundry in a very noncommittal fashion. I get the clothes and soap into the washer and turn it on, and I can usually get the wet clothes into the dryer within a few hours and turn that on. But then I'm likely to forget the whole project and days later wonder where my blue bra has gone to, and my favorite bird socks.

Sometimes they're still in the dryer, smiling up at me when I open the door. Sometimes they're wrinkling in my laundry basket where a kind renter has put them so he could dry his own laundry. For a while the embarrassment of having 20-something male renters handling my underhauls was enough to keep me on track, but lately even that has gone by the boards.

Eventually I manage to carry the basket into my bedroom, but I almost never fold the clothes any more. I dump them onto my bed, providing my cats with instant new sleeping arrangements, and dust off the cat hair when I want to wear them. At night, when I'm supposed to climb under the covers, what do I do? I just climb under the covers.

A friend says she envisions this as a layer cake: bottom sheet, then me, then top sheet and blanket, then a layer of clean laundry, and sprawling cats as the frosting...Can you imagine? All my female ancestors are spinning in their graves. I hope this is not a sign of early on-set decrepitude.

I hope it's just normal every-day sloth and torpor.

How to Avoid a Boring Life

It is truth universally acknowledged in our part of the county that the absolutely best view is to be found while waiting in line at the dump. Three or four cars back, you can see miles of the Sierra Nevada stretching south toward Yosemite. This is where you realize it's already snowed up there, or it hasn't. This is where you think of taking photos but then have to pull forward so they can assess how much you're getting rid of and therefore how much to charge you. Which, in my case yesterday, was nothing, because the broken patio umbrella and 33-year-old ironing board could be classified as metal and taken to a secret location where leaving them off was free.

I am never sorry when things turn out to be free, even though I was armed with small bills. And I'm always happy to be directed to secret locations, since much of the time I try to live my life as if I were a

Russian spy only masquerading as a middle-aged American poet.

    You should try this. Whenever you feel life has gotten unbearably boring, just imagine you aren't really yourself, but a notorious Russian spy pretending to work in the IT Department of AJA Video or as the produce manager of Safeway and your day will get immediately more interesting. How, for instance, and when are you communicating with your handlers in the mother country? Is it by two-way wrist radio like Dick Tracy in the 1950s or with your cell phone? What kind of information are you supposed to gather? Maybe it's not enough to memorize everyone's order as you pull shots at Starbucks, and you have to time the Thursday meetings of X and Y and note which table they sit at so you can set up your secret camera. Maybe if someone orders a Chai frappucino macciato al dente with no foam that's the signal for you to say "Venti or grande? Twenty-two minutes on table 5, thank you for your order, that'll be $9.50 at the window!" I mean there could be a vast network of former USSR spooks who never came in from the cold! It's very exciting, and can vastly improve a day at work if you do it right.

I picked that ironing board up off the streets
of Cambridge, Mass. on trash night in 1982, by
the way, and it gave me very good service until
recently when it stopped opening. The metal whatsis
underneath just wouldn't budge. Since I iron about
every three years, I figured I shouldn't keep it
around to clutter up the house.

This is why I was waiting in line at the dump
looking at that amazing view, and why I think it's
inevitable the dump will some day close and be
made into condominiums. It had nothing to do with
telling the metal collection department in their
secret location that Ilya Kuryakin is landing at our
municipal airport this afternoon in a Cessna 172
with green stripes. Which you did not hear from me,
I'm just an ordinary poet and life coach.

This message will self-destruct in 60 seconds.

A WHITER SHADE OF PALE

The Swans

Several years ago a friend told me that in California's Central Valley, which is about an hour from here, the rice farmers flood their fields after the harvest to provide habitat for the migrating birds that come down the Pacific Flyway. She said there were all sorts of ducks, Canada geese, Brandt's geese...but most of all there were swans.

How can you not love swans? From *The Ugly Duckling* to Swan Lake, they're a symbol of grace and perfection. They float regally in twos and threes across the moats of every castle in Europe, symbolizing luxury, but they also appear on the lakes of the poorest hamlets in upstate New York, tucking their heads under a wing and drifting as they sleep, like enormous snowy pillows. Even I love them, despite one biting my thumbnail half-off at the Palace of Fine Arts duck pond in San Francisco when I was five.

When I heard swans wintered nearby, I tried to go see them. My first attempt was foiled by a traffic jam, and we couldn't get there until after dark. It didn't seem worth stopping to me, since we couldn't see anything, but luckily my friend needed a cigarette. The minute we opened the car doors we were hit by a wave of sound: hundreds of voices gurgling, filling the night. It was amazing. It sounded like water — not the crash of waterfalls but the confluence of many little creeks. We stayed for half an hour, and the next morning I went back to see them in daylight.

There's something thrilling to me about abundance. I feel this way looking at pumpkins lying in the fields in October, and mile after mile of blossoming almond groves in early April. One is great, ten is better, but so many you can't count them is *really* exciting! There were probably 10,000 swans in those rice fields, dots of white as far as the eye could see. I counted 300 in the first field I came to. They sit and sleep and lumber awkwardly in the shallow water, always making their gurgling calls. They lift in pairs and dozens to circle overhead for a while, disappearing at some angles and then gilded white and gold in the sun at others. They fly in vees to try other locations. When they land, there's a lot

of precarious flapping before the splash and then
they fold into that elegant long-necked silhouette as
if they had never had an ungraceful moment.

    The swans are here from Thanksgiving to the
middle of January. Then they migrate somewhere
else. When I'm feeling insane about the relentless
materialism of an American Christmas, I go visit the
swans. I want you to go, too. Take your binoculars,
camera, mittens, and a thermos of hot cider. Bring
your kids and your father-in-law. Forget about gravy
and piles of presents under the tree.

    Instead, stand in the stark landscape of winter
and gaze at a different Christmas miracle: swans by
the murmuring acre.

Reindeer

An e-mail has been circulating recently, suggesting Santa's reindeer are female, because male reindeer shed their antlers in the fall, and females don't shed theirs until April. This is supposedly why Santa makes it to everyone's house in one night: female reindeer aren't afraid to ask for directions.

Like many other urban, or in this case arctic legends, the story is plausible but not incontrovertible. Female reindeer do shed their antlers in spring — so Santa's could be female. But most males don't shed until early December, and the younger ones are often later. Santa's team could be teenaged males, or late-shedding adult males, or even coed.

I don't know why anyone would name a male reindeer Vixen, and Dasher, Dancer, Prancer, Comet, Cupid, Donner, and Blitzen all seem fairly unisex to me. These monikers come from the poem "A Visit from St. Nicholas," now universally known by its first line: "Twas the night before Christmas," written by Clement Clarke Moore in 1822. Rudolph is the only clearly male name, and that was invented as a Montgomery Ward promotional gimmick in 1939.

I love Christmas — even though I'm single and regret not having my own nuclear family to enjoy it with — even though this year my cats are still young enough to take down in minutes any tree that I might be foolhardy enough to put up. I love Christmas lights, glittery decorations, tinsel, eggnog, wrapping paper and ribbon, and the smell of pine, balsam, and fir. I love standing around a piano with my friends to sing carols, even the most ridiculous of them, like Rudolph the Red-Nosed Reindeer.

Real reindeer live wild in Canada and Alaska. They've been domesticated in Eurasia for about 7000 years, which is longer than the horse. They live almost exclusively above the Arctic Circle — not at the North Pole but in Norway, Sweden, Finland, and the Kola Peninsula of Russia — herded by the still-nomadic Lapps, a.k.a. Sami. Their hooves are large for their body size, working a little like snowshoes, and the edges act as blades to facilitate walking on ice. The shovel-like design also helps with swimming and foraging for lichen.

Here is my reindeer story. I once ventured to Lapland in June. Leaning over the railing of the boat I'd been traveling on for a week, at about three in the morning — in other words, broad daylight — I saw a log jam up ahead, followed by two dinghies. As the boat got closer, the logs looked more like a huge tangle of branches...closer still they turned out to be antlers. Below them was a froth of white from thousands of hooves churning the water. Lapps, in their traditional blue costumes with all the rick-rack, waved and shouted from the dinghies, motoring back and forth, herding their reindeer across from the mainland to summer pasture.

Have yourself a merry little Christmas, and remember to keep your eye out for miracles. Male or female. Reindeer or otherwise. They're everywhere.

Duck Potholders & *Galoises*

The week between Christmas and New Year's
has always been one of my favorites. Life goes into
delectable slow motion. Despite a few crazy people
exchanging presents they didn't like for something
else, or scooping up wrapping paper on sale to
use next year, everyone's all shopped out for the
moment. The advertisers have done their best, and
are briefly silent. No glossy catalogs arrive in the
mail. *The New Yorker* and *Vogue* are slim again,
after their seasonal bloating. The incessant din of
supply and demand is hushed as commerce takes an
all-too-brief annual break from its vigorous and wily
efforts to part each of us from our last remaining
dollar.

The kids aren't in school and people are out
of town, so traffic thins to a trickle. Refrigerators
bristle with leftovers and no one has to run to the
grocery store: we just invent new and ever-more-

bizarre concoctions out of celery, yams, and gravy. That is, when we even bother to eat. Enough eating takes place in the first three weeks of December to sustain most of us until Easter.

What this time of year always makes me think of is the lull in those old black-and-white French movies after a torrid sex scene, when the two lovers lean back into their pillows and light cigarettes. Maybe they talk a little, or give each other a look, but mostly it's just smoke curling up from their two *Gauloises*, and a little background music.

I myself woke up yesterday to a rainy day and snuggled in bed for the first time in my life to watch a video before breakfast. This was so outlandish that I had to race around afterward and do five or six productive things just to prove I hadn't completely lost my moral fibers. Then a sudden attack of sewing came over me and I got out some blue fabric with ducks on it that I've been meaning to make into potholders for years. Five years, to be exact. Instead of creating new pot holders from scratch, I covered the two ratty ones I had, and now they're so elegant and pristine I hesitate to use them.

After the manic stitching fit, I calmed down again and sat on the sofa reading one of my Christmas presents: a biography of the poet Anne

Bradstreet. In between forays out to the woodpile and stir-frying Turkey Surprise, I've been dipping into this book all week. I've also been wearing my new Xmas socks, and creating my own lattes with a fabulous milk-fizzling gizmo. If it weren't for making a living, this would be the life, I tell you!

There's something delicious about not being on a schedule. That kind of goofing-around time is incredibly nourishing. As well as covering potholders, which was about two-thousand-nine-hundred-and-twelfth on my to-do list, I had enough spaciousness in my head to write a poem.

If you've had a languorous week like this also, remember it when the time comes to think up New Year's resolutions, and don't make any.

Balloon Up Your Nose!

It began with a cold, the kind most of us get every winter: headache, congestion, coughing, sneezing, post-nasal drip, and it's gone in seven days no matter what you take to make it end sooner. In our town, a few of us also got nose bleeds. I got six small ones, and then as my symptoms subsided, I got one that lasted an hour and a half. My EMT-trained friends taught me you don't lie on the floor with an ice pack under your neck the way we did as kids. You sit on the couch upright, or lean forward, possibly over the sink, and hold the bridge of your nose tightly for 20 minutes.

I hadn't had a bad nosebleed in years. I'd forgotten how the human head likes to bleed, and how red the blood is. The verbs "gush," and "spray," come to mind, as well as the adjective "ginormous" and the noun "clot." I used up two boxes of tissues.

But then it was over, my cold got better, and I went about my business: bringing in firewood for the stove, not drinking enough water, eating very little kale, and so forth. Two nights later, I woke to a blood-drenched pillow. That was a dreadful mess to clean, but I stopped it myself. The next day, however, the bleeding started again and never ceased. I drove one-handed to the ER, where a nice doc who couldn't have been older than 12 cauterized my nose and then "packed" it, which is what they call the balloon trick.

These balloons look perfectly innocent, although twice as long as a human nose. This is because there are caves in our heads, with room to stuff things in. I should have been forewarned by the doctor's wince as he pushed this item all the way into my orifice. That was bad, but tolerable. Then, as is typical of balloons, there was inflation. A syringe. A tube drooping out of my nostril. And they tape the tube to the side of your face, so you can't pretend something isn't terribly wrong.

I hope you're drinking a glass of water now, and wondering where in the attic your humidifier is stored.

I had a few anxiety attacks, but after 48 hours was allowed to take the thing out myself, had a

blissful day, and then, in a public restaurant with
a friend, bled all over my dinner salad. Back to
the ER. Five days this time. Despair, desperation,
homicidal thoughts, abject self-pity…Extremely
kind people took care of me, which was amazing and
completely undeserved.

But we think it worked. I haven't seen a drop of
blood in a week. The dull all-consuming ache in my
sinuses is gone. I'm so grateful I want to cry. The
ER bill is going make me actually cry, but I hope I
can still be grateful as I pay it down a few dollars a
month for the rest of my natural life.

A Whiter Shade of Pale

Well, It's been a complicated morning.

First I was getting ready to write about the Charlie Hebdo massacre in France, wondering how to talk about the fact that I believe in free speech but I don't like meanness, and how satire and ridicule can be so mean. Not that anyone should ever kill people over this, but it's still no fun to be the butt of jokes.

Then I was trying to figure out how to talk about Paris and Nigeria together, and make some sense out of the public response to one and the general lack of interest among first world countries about the second, but I realized that I had no idea what was behind the Boko Haram attack. I started to do some research on it, sitting at my local cafe drinking a latte, squinting at my phone.

That was when the call came in saying our friend Ed had died during the night. Ed who used to sit in the afternoons where I sit in the mornings: at the back counter of Sierra Mountain Coffee Roasters, middle chair, where you can see all the action both behind and in front of the cash register. Ed with the fabulous southern accent, on whom I had a crush for precisely three weeks in 2007, which ended as abruptly and mysteriously as it had begun.

After that news, I couldn't concentrate on anything, and came home to prepare for my first and only life-coaching client of the day. I am working out of my house at the moment, so the bathroom needs to be spotless, the black cat-hair brushed off the green sofa, and a few boxes removed from the living room to somewhere out of sight. The cleaning part was easy, and so was the coaching part, because my client today is so ready for change that all I do is suggest something and she takes off after the idea like a greyhound.

As I was scrubbing the toilet bowl I began to hum "A Whiter Shade of Pale," and realized that I'm getting Boko Haram, the extremist group in Africa, mixed up with Procol Harum, the 1960s British rock band. "Boko Haram" means "Western education is forbidden" in Nigerian. "Procol Harum" was the name of a Burmese cat belonging to a friend of the band's original manager, Guy Stevens.

By this point, the idea that I'm supposed to write an essay for the radio that will make any kind of sense seems incredibly unlikely. However, I still have two hours before the recording time. Maybe I'll be able to think of something.

My coaching client ended up not using the bathroom, so cleaning it was perhaps wasted effort except that it makes me cheerful to see it sparkle. I was reminded of a quote from Wendell Berry that was going around Facebook late last night.

"Be joyful even though you've considered the facts."

This seems like a pretty tall order today, but I'm game. What do you think? Shall we try it?

The Watusi

Sometimes I sit around and think about the difference between loneliness and solitude. Why is it that one night I'm just delighted to be alone, reading or puttering, stoking the fire and listening to rain hit the tin water-heater vent, while the next I'm irascible and despairing in the same exact circumstances, sure I'll die of loneliness? Not even the cats can save me — *they* have each *other* and I'm a solitary miserable human with no source of solace in this life. It gets a little melodramatic as you can see, but it feels all too real when I'm in it.

Long, long ago, my family used to drive from San Francisco to Carmel on Friday nights to spend the weekend. We'd leave after supper, the three oldest kids lengthwise in the folded-down back seat of my mom's white Buick like sardines, and the youngest horizontally at our feet. Our parents hoped we'd sleep for the two-hour ride but I rarely did. I tried to snag the passenger-side spot behind Mom, because then when we drove down Broadway to the freeway on-ramp, I could look up and see the go-go dancer.

Did other cities have a girl dancing high above their Red-Light district in 1967? Certainly not Boston, the only place we went. She was in a little phone booth-sized cubicle at the top of a pole several storeys higher than the club she advertised. She had to climb the pole herself — you could see the ladder of bars for her feet — wearing those calf-high white boots that defined the era and a little bathing-suit-like outfit with lots of fringe. She stayed up there all alone and danced, a teaser for the sexy goings-on below. I don't remember if there was music playing as we passed and I don't know if she had any piped in. I just see her through my wide twelve-year-old eyes doing the Watusi, the Pony, and the Swim, lit like a lighthouse beacon above the street and getting smaller and smaller as we merged with Friday night traffic on 101. When we came home on Sunday nights the booth was empty.

I think some of the loneliness of my childhood got wrapped up in the image of this girl — a strange but potent symbol of the adulthood I was fast approaching. I always wondered if she liked it by herself looking at the lights of the city, or if she was lonely. Was she delighted not to be stripping every night and groped by strange men, or was she missing the tips and the camaraderie of the other girls who worked there? (In 1967 we still called women "girls"). Did she take cigarette breaks? Was she afraid of heights?

You may have noticed that the human condition is a mercurial thing — all our lives we negotiate its ups and downs, its pain, elation, general random unfairness, and blinding good luck. Some days this is easier than others. When I get so lonely I think it will kill me, I remember that mysterious girl in the white boots, her knees lifting and her fringe swaying from side to side. "At least," I say to myself by way of comfort, "I'm not half-naked, thirty feet high in a plexiglass phone booth doing the Watusi!"

Ursus Californiensis

Earlier today I was sitting at my favorite café thinking about writing. Various people came over to talk to me and an hour later the page was still blank. I'd done a lot of laughing, which is always good for a person, and imbibed my morning caffeine — right now a requirement for sanity — but nothing on my mental to-do list was checked off.

Next I drove over to the 10-Minute Oil Change and sat at one of their tables for the 45 minutes it took to do my car. One item crossed off the list, and I committed the list to paper, which was kind of fun and made me feel productive. This is a delusion, of course.

The rain had stopped and the sky turned that bright gray it gets when the sun is hiding behind only a thin layer of clouds. I looked out the Oil Change lobby plate glass for a while, watching the weather. This was not on my to-do list, but it should have been. Humans, especially poets, need to watch the world in action, from spark plug to thunderhead. It's how we make sense of our lives, but no one remembers this. I think January, the slowest, most self-effacing month of the year, was invented as a reminder.

My next stop was the vet's office for worm pills. Five out of five cats have been chomping up gophers, voles, lizards, and — I hate to say it — one bunny. Plus, it's tick season. All of this leads to tape worms, for whom I harbor complete disgust. It's no fun to cram a pill down anyone's throat, but at least it's quick and I'm well-practiced. Each cat hates me until dinner time, and then we're cool.

I don't have any coaching clients today, nor writing deadlines, edits due, blog posts to think up. It's just me, January, and rain. I could and possibly should write a poem about this. Or I could build a fire instead, eat some soup, and take a nap, thereby bowing at the altar of my inner California black bear (*Ursus americanus californiensis*). Taking pleasure in moving, eating, snoozing, and laughing honors the animals we truly are, and we really don't do it enough.

I'm not sure whether bears think, or what they might be thinking about. Honey? Salmon? They do write, though, on trees with their enormous curved claws, scraping into the bark a version of what we're all trying to say, beneath our plain or fancy syntax: "I was here. I exist."

Today, I can feel that I exist.

I'm smiling into my rearview as I drive the last miles home. I just remembered my favorite motto, something I heard spoken on the radio decades ago by an old blues musician and have never been able to trace. He was laughing at the interviewer, in a great deep bear-like voice:

"Start out slow," he said, and paused. "And then…ease off."

Borrowing Other Mothers

All my life, I've been borrowing other people's mothers. Usually they had no idea, although I'm sure some figured it out, and sometimes I told them. In grade school, Joan's mother Ilse, an Austrian-born psychiatrist much older than my own mom, served as an intimidating example of the genre. I loved her from a distance, exotic in tailored suits, elegant gray hair, and foreign accent. She taught Joan and me to make apple strudel from scratch, and eat salad at the end of dinner instead of the beginning. She was appalled that my parents let me walk the eight San Francisco blocks to their house by myself, and insisted on driving me home.

Peggy's mom Doris got me through high school. When I couldn't stand the tension in our 15-room Victorian, I went over there, where three tall kids and Doris lived in 700 square feet and wool was always being dyed on the stove with onion skins

or some kind of jam was in process, scarlet runner
beans grew up the fence, people sang, and frisbees
flew around the driveway. I can't remember one
conversation I had with Doris, but the welcome I felt
in her presence, as well as her no-nonsense approach
to the kids not doing their homework, are still
lodged in my memory. Watching someone's mother
work all day at a job and raise three kids by herself
while singing was a revelation.

When I went back East to college, mothers
were the last thing on my mind. I had aunts
and a grandmother nearby, and was practicing
independence in any case. But one Easter I went
to a party at Julie's family home, north of Boston.
From their big house overlooking the Atlantic,
about 40 of us went on a long, complicated outdoor
hunt, not for Easter eggs but for painted rocks. It
was freezing and windy but very bright, the sun
sparkling off the ocean, and Julie's mother Jane
was quintessentially warm, calling us back into the
house for lunch.

I've probably seen Jane only ten times in
the intervening four decades, but her sense of
rootedness and deep curiosity has led me to hold
her in my mind as a beacon. How she could stand,
gracious in the eye of that storm of her rowdy

children and all their rowdy friends, doling out food and napkins, keeping the dogs away from the ham, and still notice an individual, struck me as something to aspire to.

I loved my own mom, and consciously took on lots of her characteristics, too. But borrowing mothers who were different from her, whom I didn't have to defend against their own choices and sadness, enriches my life no end.

I found out just now on Google that Ilse lived to be 96. I haven't been in touch since she sent a lovely letter when my father died, 30 years ago. But Doris still sings, up in Washington State, and Jane writes me kind notes about these radio essays, which arrive in her e-mail in-box at that same house on the cliff overlooking the Atlantic.

Glass Houses

Yesterday, I looked at a street sign and decided to disobey it. I don't know what came over me — I was late meeting a friend for dinner, but not enough to matter. The road seemed quite empty. It wasn't dusk yet but the light had softened, something that often makes me feel as though everything's going to be alright.

So I turned left in front of the *No Left Turn* sign pulling out of a gas station, and was immediately in trouble. A car came in on my left wanting to make the light, but I was in the way. Another came around the corner on my right and began to accelerate, which is what you do at this intersection. And a truck materialized at the post office exit right in front of me, a large black apparition ready to pull into the spot I was aiming for.

I threw up my hands, mouthed "I'm sorry!!!" and while they all waited, scowling, I finished the turn and went on my way. I didn't patch out and I didn't drive at a snail's pace either. I proceeded normally, as if nothing had ever been wrong and I was a perfectly excellent driver. Like many miscreants before me, when the truck zoomed past I did not turn my head to see if he was cursing.

After I got home from dinner, driving exactly the speed limit the whole way in penance, I turned on my computer. All over social media there were photos of a white Cadillac Escalade literally on top of an Audi parked on the main street of my town. The Audi had smashed into a VW which in turn had rear-ended a Mercedes, and all of this had happened on a hill, but facing *up* the hill, which means there had to have been some speed involved. Along with photos, people had posted video from several different angles of a tow truck winching the Escalade sideways and upright to get it back on solid ground.

When I made my bone-headed left-turn decision, I wasn't drunk or high. I wasn't even tired. I was feeling inconvenienced, since to obey the exit signs no matter how I did it was going to take me blocks out of my way. I had the common American delusion that posted signs don't always apply to me. It was lucky the three drivers I blockaded had good reflexes and weren't texting anybody.

I hear the toddler in the Escalade wasn't hurt, and the crunched conga line of empty parked cars didn't hit anyone on the sidewalk. The driver, also unharmed, was taken in on a DUI. Lots of righteousness flew around on social media, in which, needless to say, I did not take part. I may be dumb enough to disobey street signs, but I'm not so dumb as to think I should then offer anyone else driving advice.

Humans are made up mostly of water, stardust, and self-involvement. Our main lifetime recreation is making mistakes. Even if you've never once done anything wrong — and pardon me while I raise an eyebrow — it really is tempting Fate to cast the first stone.

Valentine Grumblings

So now the year swings around again to Valentine's Day, that Hallmark holiday promoted within an inch of its life to sell chocolate, red roses, and, more recently, extremely small items of see-through underwear.

When I'm single on Valentine's Day, I wonder if it's a plot to remind the unattached that they're unloved. Red doily hearts in store windows make me resentful and crabby. And the part of me that wanted to be a ballerina when I was 9 and still occasionally dreams of silk wedding gowns feels bereft and then manipulated. I am sometimes tempted, at this time of year, to ram my grocery cart into the candy display and watch the whole thing collapse. Or to drive strategically through a puddle close to the curb as a happy-looking couple is strolling by, in order to douse them. I know this is not adult behavior, but there you have it.

When I'm coupled up on Valentine's Day, the holiday seems ridiculous. Why arbitrarily designate a day for love when so many days are full of love, and also chocolate? Why put obligation on your partner in this artificial way? What a set-up for expectations and inevitable disappointment.

It also drives me nuts how narrowly imagined the chocolate and roses thing is. It's such an enormous cliché, repeated doggedly year after year. Why not strike a blow for freedom, break out of the darn See's chocolates box and at least send *yellow* roses! Use your imagination! Give your beloved jasmine and gingersnaps or orchids and Chinese plum sauce — things that are equally sensuous but not so familiar. Or better yet, get creative and *make* something. Write a poem to your sweetheart — or, if poems terrify you, just make a list of what you love about him or her. And be specific — paying attention is a clear sign of love. List all sorts of things: the grace with which she lifts a coffee cup, the efficient dispatch he brings to packing a car's trunk. Describe the sexy things, too, but don't limit your list to them — intimacy exists in so many surprising places.

I should admit that despite all this grumbling, I love a romantic gesture as much as the next person. I just think they should be inventive. I gave my best valentine (so far) one year when I was living in Cambridge. It snowed three feet on February 13th, and at midnight I went out in my snow boots, wrapped to the gills in muffler, hat and mittens, to find my boyfriend Denis's white Volkswagen. I was armed with five tubes of lipstick and a box of Kleenex. I spent an hour — the snow falling lightly around me, in that timeless hush snow brings — applying the different colors of lipstick and wiping spots on his car clean of winter grime so I could leave kissprints. My lips didn't freeze to the metal surface because lipstick is sort of greasy, which was also good since it stopped the snow from washing the prints away.

    I kissed that car 50 times, and Denis said later it overheated for weeks afterwards.

The Gates

I did something wilder than usual last week, I took a red-eye to New York to see Christo's Gates Project. This sort of thing is not in my budget, but I had planned ahead, so I had the dough saved up. I met two friends there whom I never get to see, was completely transported by the Gates, and it taught me all over again that a poet needs to leave town and look at strangeness once in a while, in service to her art.

Christo's Gates in Central Park are not like garden gates, those waist-high interruptions in a picket fence. They're portals — enormous orange door frames for the house of a giant — and imbued with all the mythology that metaphor implies.

If you haven't seen the photos yet or watched *60 Minutes*, each gate is 16 feet tall, made of three pieces of steel encased in orange plastic – two tall verticals with a cross bar at the top. From that top bar hangs a swath of sturdy orange rip-stop nylon, pleated at first and then loose, ending seven feet above the ground, so that everyone except basketball teams can walk underneath them. I didn't see any basketball teams, but just about everyone else showed up: walkers, bikers, skateboarders, roller skaters, little kids on their dads' shoulders reaching up to swat the fabric, old couples in wool coats and orange mufflers. Everyone seemed to wear orange if they had any.

Have I mentioned that there are *7500* of these things, arching over 23 miles of paths in Central Park? The sheer number gave the project a glorious lunacy. From any given point you could see at least three or four Gates, and most of the time you could see more like 200, angling off crazily under the trees.

I walked the length of the park with my friends, riffing on what they reminded us of — curtains in windows, laundry on the line, rows of ballet dancers, prayer flags. The wind blew some of them but not others, so it seemed as though the whole regiment was in motion — like a slow-moving Chinese New Year dragon. The volunteers tried to tell us the color was saffron, but it wasn't as yellow or as dark as that. It was a true Cal-Trans-truck orange, vivid under blue sky, luminous under gray.

We fell into conversation with lots of people — a tiny French woman, elegant in a full-length (orange) down coat told me they were a gift to the city, and a burly young man in a sweatshirt growled that they were OK. Some people were crying, as I had cried when I first saw them, although I couldn't tell you why. Maybe it's the grandness of the gesture that's so moving — like coming upon acres of poppies or a huge pod of whales.

Mostly everyone looked at the Gates in wonder — talking a mile a minute, since it was New York — and smiled at one another. As we left, a cop on the corner said to his partner: *Look at all these people! The city hasn't been alive like this since the towers fell.*

Wedding Bells

The thing about being a wedding officiant is that they really can't get anywhere without you. I'm not usually late to things, and I'd hate to be late to someone's wedding ceremony, but knowing I'm this vital to the proceedings is kind of relaxing. Which is good, because usually at a wedding everyone around you is the opposite of relaxed. Excited to the point of possibly throwing up? Yes. Tense, intense, and overwhelmed with detail? Yes. And sometimes also sad, confused, lonely, and — if your recent ex- will be there with her or his new, younger, partner — possibly enraged.

Sometimes I run across an older relative of the groom who's as relaxed as I am. Usually he has come to be supportive, likes a shindig, is glad he's not one of the principals, and doesn't really mind what happens. Bouquets can come apart, cake tables collapse, entire tents fall on everyone's head and he's just amused.

I should probably find someone like that if I
ever decide to marry, but then he'd be one of the
principals and I wouldn't be the officiant — we'd
both tense up and it would probably end in tears.

Today, I'm not marrying anyone — the wedding
is tomorrow. Today the groom's brother, who runs a
tour company, is taking us to visit many of the sights
around Seattle. It is currently pouring with rain but
we'll be safe and dry on a very small tour bus.

I'm staying at an elegant and well-known hotel
right on the water. I have a first floor, waterside
room with a balcony. It's not quite like standing
next to a swimming pool, but it's pretty close: even a
wimp such as myself wouldn't be afraid to dive from
this height. But as it is February, and raining, I've
decided not to. Also the swells are four or five feet
high. And, you know, Puget Sound is full of orcas.
"Wedding Officiant Bitten in Half by Killer Whale"
would probably sell newspapers, but is not a good
omen for marriage.

Instead, I'll look through the sliding glass door
at that moving water and be glad I'm not on a
cruise ship requiring intravenous Dramamine or
something stronger. I will not nervously add oceanic
metaphors to the vows. I'll put on my scarf and
raincoat and calmly walk the three miles from my

room to the lobby to wait for the very small tour bus.

Have I mentioned how much I love the couple I'll be marrying, and how much I love my life? Who else gets invited to marry people in the Space Needle with a crown of roses on her head? I feel incredibly lucky, which makes me want to spread happiness as far as the eye can see. So, dearly beloved, using the power vested in me by the State of Washington, I now pronounce you a wonderful person.

After obtaining permission, you may kiss whomever you wish.

Acknowledgements

I thanked many people in my first two books of essays. I did not thank any cats. This omission was noticed in certain quarters and a request has been made to remedy the disastrous oversight, even if thanking one's cats might expose a person to ridicule and humiliation since it's the height of horrible middle-aged single female clichés. For the sake of love and gratitude, I'm happy to be thought absurd. Dear Sid, Gracie, Black Jack, India, Mimi, Sprocket, Emma, Maggie, Calico Sister, Ajax, Oliver, Red Jack, Skeezix, Angus, Seamus, Fergus, Jerry, Ivan, Winjin, and Buttercup, thank you for making my life easier to bear.

The individual essays in this book originally aired as commentary on the News Hour of community radio station KVMR in Nevada City, CA or on KQED's California Report between 2004 and

2016 (© Molly Fisk). Download recent commentary for public radio airplay in a strict 4-minute format by contacting Paul Emery at kvmr.org. There is no charge. This material is brought to you by the author and by KVMR 89.5 FM Nevada City, California through a grant from the Corporation for Public Broadcasting. Selected essays in this book, some under different titles, have appeared on womensvoicesforchange.com.

About the Author

Molly Fisk is the author of the essay collections *Using Your Turn Signal Promotes World Peace* and *Blow-Drying a Chicken*, and the poetry collections, *The More Difficult Beauty, Listening to Winter, Terrain* (co-author) and *Salt Water Poems*. Her essays have aired weekly as part of the News Hour of KVMR-FM Nevada City, CA since 2005.

Fisk has been awarded grants by the National Endowment for the Arts, the California Arts Council, and the Corporation for Public Broadcasting. She's currently Poet Laureate of KVMR in Nevada City and Hell's Backbone Grill in Boulder, Utah.

Fisk works as a life coach in the Skills for Change tradition and owns Poetry Boot Camp (poetrybootcamp.com). Visit her at mollyfisk.com.

To order signed and inscribed copies of *Houston, We Have a Possum*, or any of Molly Fisk's other books, please visit www.mollyfisk.com/writing.

www.ingramcontent.com/pod-product-compliance
Lightning Source LLC
Chambersburg PA
CBHW020110020526
44112CB00033B/1138